# SMM7 QUESTIONS & ANSWERS

by

## John Davidson FRICS

is a Director of Cyril Sweett and the Honorary Queries Secretary for the Standing Joint Committee for the Standard Method of Measurement

and

## Paul Hambleton BSc FRICS

is a practising Quantity Surveyor with over 25 years' industry experience

RICS BOOKS

# Acknowledgements

The authors and publishers wish to thank the Standing Joint Committee for the Standard Method of Measurement for the use of material from the *SMM7 Standard Method of Measurement of Building Works* and the *SMM7 Measurement Code*.

John Davidson would also like to thank his employer, Cyril Sweett Ltd, for their support during the writing of this book.

Published by RICS Business Services Limited
a wholly owned subsidiary of
The Royal Institution of Chartered Surveyors
under the RICS Books imprint
Surveyor Court
Westwood Business Park
Coventry CV4 8JE
UK
www.ricsbooks.com

ISBN 978 1 84219 228 0

ISBN (prior to January 2007) 1 84219 228 0

Typeset in Great Britain by Columns Design Ltd, Reading, Berks

Printed in Great Britain by Cromwell Press, Trowbridge, Wiltshire

# Contents

# Introduction

This book *SMM7 Questions & Answers* is a companion volume to the seventh edition of the *Standard Method of Measurement* (SMM7) and the *SMM7 Measurement Code*. It has been written to try to assist in the interpretation of some of the more complex areas of measurement and work description.

The authors hope that it will eliminate many of the arguments and disputes, and explain some of the more common misunderstandings which can arise on construction projects due to differences of interpretation. This text uses questions sent to the Standing Joint Committee (SJC) and their responses on live issues. For ease of understanding by the reader, questions and responses have been paraphrased and, where appropriate, combined with other similar questions.

This book utilises diagrams in certain cases to clarify the question or the answer in relation to identify with the *Standard Method of Measurement* text. The book follows the structure of SMM7 and its component chapters. However, because the book is based on actual questions submitted to the SJC for SMM7, not all sections are covered here.

It is also important to recognise that SMM7 and this book both deal with the measurement and description of construction work. Among the queries received by the SJC there are a number which do not fall within the committee's remit; such as queries on landfill tax, on valuation methods for variations, or on actual rates set for jobs. These issues are not discussed in this text.

## How to use this book and its general layout

The book is written in the same sequence as the *Standard Method of Measurement* (SMM). The chapters are those as set out in the SMM. To avoid confusion, the first section annotation is used for the questions and answers contained thereunder, the other headings listed in section are taken as being referred to by the first heading annotation. For example:

## F20 Natural stone rubble walling

## F21 Natural stone ashlar walling/dressings

## F22 Cast stone ashlar walling/dressings

| INFORMATION PROVIDED | MEASUREMENT RULES | DEFINITION RULES | COVERAGE RULES | SUPPLEMENTARY INFORMATION |
|---|---|---|---|---|
| P1, P2, etc. | M1, M2, etc. | D1, D2, etc. | C1, C2, etc. | S1, S2, etc. |
| CLASSIFICATION TABLE | | | | |

The questions and answers in this section are referenced as F20.1.1.1.1, Measurement Rule F20.M1, etc., for simplicity even if they may be specific to the other headings (i.e. F21, F22). Where detailed numbers such as F20.1.*.1 are used they refer to the numbered items in the Classification Table. (Note that '.*.' corresponds to a blank column.)

Occasionally a question is included in more than one section, typically where the Work Section in the answer is different from that raised in the question.

# Important notes

Some SMM7 Work Sections and subsections were renumbered and new Work Sections introduced in the 1998 Revision. These were Work Sections C, D, E F, G, H J, K, l, M, Q, and R.

All SMM7 references refer to the current edition, i.e. the *Seventh Edition Revised 1998*, incorporating Amendments 1 and 2.

The interpretation of the rules of SMM7 are those of the authors but are based on replies made under the auspices of the SJC.

All answers given in this book assume strict interpretation of the rules of measurement contained within SMM7. This may mean that some answers appear to be extremely pedantic. Surveyors are free to measure any item of work in any other way they may think appropriate provided they insert an explanatory note or qualification in the Bill(s) of quantities clearly describing their intentions.

NOTE: No work can be deemed included, irrespective of what the measurement rules say, unless it can be seen on the drawings or understood from the specification or by reference to a catalogue or other standard specification, such as a British Standard, that can be easily obtained by the estimator when pricing the Bills of quantities.

# Symbols and abbreviations

The following symbols and abbreviations are used in this book.

| AI | = | architect's instruction |
|----|---|---|
| BoQ(s) | = | Bill(s) of quantities (other common abbreviations are BofQ and BQ) |
| BWIC | = | builders' work in connection |
| DPC | = | damp-proof course |
| DPM | = | damp-proof membrane |
| EO | = | extra over |
| EWS | = | earth work support |
| h | = | hour |
| kg | = | kilogramme |
| m | = | metre |
| $m^2$ | = | square metre |
| $m^3$ | = | cubic metre |
| mm | = | millimetre |
| NBS | = | National Building Specification |
| n.e. or n/e | = | not exceeding |
| nr | = | number |
| o/a | = | overall |
| pc sum | = | prime cost sum |
| prov sum | = | provisional sum |
| QS | = | quantity surveyor |
| t | = | tonne |
| > | = | exceeding |
| ⩾ | = | equal to or exceeding |
| ⩽ | = | not exceeding |
| < | = | less than |
| % | = | percentage |
| .*. | = | blank column |

# Introduction

The book references rules using the Work Section and Rule number, e.g. Measurement Rule F10.M1.

Classification Table Rules are referenced by the Work Section then column numbers from left to right, e.g. F10.1.1.1, H10.3.*.1, Y10.9.1.

Publications referred to regularly in this book are abbreviated as follows:

**SMM7**  *Standard Method of Measurement of Building Works* (7th edition), revised 1998 incorporating Amendments 1 and 2 (May 2000)

**Measurement Code**  *SMM7 Measurement Code: A Code of Procedure for Measurement of Building Works*, revised 1998 incorporating Amendments 1 and 2 (January 2000)

**CAWS**  *Common Arrangement for Building Works* (2nd edition), 1998

# General Rules

## 1 Introduction

▶ Do departures from the rules of SMM7 need to be specifically referred to if made when preparing a BoQ?

Yes, all departures must be clearly set out in the BoQ.

## 2 Use of the tabulated rules

▶ If the employer requires such items as spare carpet tiles, raised floor panels or suspended ceiling tiles to be provided should specific items be measured? SMM7 appears silent on this matter.

Yes, General Rule 2.5 reminds us that the rules do not cover every event therefore, in accordance with General Rule 11.1, the surveyor must adapt rules for similar work accordingly.

▶ If relevant information is not given in the BoQ description, whether as part of the worded description, by a unique cross reference or by a drawing reference, does this constitute a Bill error?

Yes, General Rules 2 and 4 set out what minimum information must be given when composing Bill descriptions.

## 4 Descriptions

▶ A Bill description relies on a reference to a drawing to describe a composite item. After tender a conflict is discovered between the drawn information and the Bill description. Which takes priority?

The drawn information will always take priority. If a discrepancy is found in a Bill item it must be remeasured in accordance with the drawing or the executed work.

▶ Where drawings are being relied upon to define the location, scope and extent of work to be included as a provisional sum in a BoQ, must these drawings be specifically referred to in the description of the provisional sum or is it sufficient for these drawings to be listed only as tender drawings?

General Rule 4.2 is quite specific in requiring a cross reference to be given in the description when using drawn information in lieu of a written description.

▶ Can a 'unique and precise' cross reference be given as part of the information required by General Rule 4?

Yes.

A 'saluting base' is measured as a composite item with reference to a drawing. It is to be constructed mainly of stainless steel and glass. Is it reasonable to assume the 'plate glass' to be included in BoQ item which reads 'stainless steel saluting base, Drawing No. [XX]'? There is no mention of glass in the remainder of the BoQ description and very limited reference to glass on the drawing.

No, the item does not comply with the requirements of General Rules 4.2 and 9.1.

General Rule 4.2 does not allow the aggregation of a number of measured items which are otherwise required to be measured separately. Also the construction shown on the drawing would not be considered as a composite item as it would be difficult to construct and assemble off site and re-assemble on site.

# 9 Composite items

A BoQ description reads as follows – 'Timber framed laylight as specification Clause L40.211; wrot softwood; double glazed units; all decoration; as Architect's drawings X and Y'. Should the BoQ description be held to include an aluminium rooflight because it is shown on the drawings?

No, General Rule 4.2 does not permit the aggregation of items. The BoQ item has not been qualified and therefore cannot be held to contain anything other than the timber frame. The use of a unique specification reference does not automatically mean that every item contained in the specification item is to be taken as being measured in the Bill description.

The BoQ description and specification reference make no reference to an aluminium rooflight within the timber framed laylight. The drawings do show an aluminium rooflight.

General Rule 9.1 defines composite items and this Bill description does not comply with that definition.

# 10 Procedure where the drawn and specification information required by these rules is not available

Can a provisional sum be described as 'defined' if not all of the information is given as required by General Rule 10.3?

No, all relevant information required by General Rule 10.3 must be given for a provisional sum to be described as 'defined'.

If a provisional sum is 'undefined', should the tenderer be held to have made allowances in the Preliminaries for programming, planning, etc?

No, see General Rule 10.6 and Clause 10, page 13 of the *Measurement Code*.

If a provisional sum is 'undefined', must the contractor allow for percentage profit if there is such an item included in the BoQ for a sum to be inserted?

Yes, as long as General Rules 10.2 to 10.6 inclusive are properly qualified in the BoQ. Normally the amount given to a provisional sum includes an allowance for 'profit'.

▶ What is the difference between a defined and an undefined provisional sum and how should the sums be calculated?

For a provisional sum to be defined, the Bill description must contain all the information required by General Rules 10.3(a)–(d) inclusive. If the provisional sum does not include even one of these criteria then it must be classed as an undefined provisional sum.

When calculating how much an undefined provisional sum should be, the surveyor must make due allowance for all costs that a contractor might incur when expending that provisional sum, including all costs associated with items listed in General Rule 4.6(a)–(g) inclusive and costs for programming, planning and pricing the preliminaries as General Rule 10.6.

If the provisional sum descriptions meet the criteria set out in General Rule 10.3, the contractor is not entitled to any additional costs for preliminaries.

A defined provisional sum amount will include sums for all costs associated with labour, materials, assembling and fitting, plant, waste, square cutting, establishment charges, overheads and profit as described in General Rule 4.6(a)–(g) inclusive.

Clause 10.4 of the General Rules states that 'the contractor will be deemed to have made due allowance in programming, planning and pricing Preliminaries'.

The rules of Section A54 of the Preliminaries section of SMM7 do not provide for the inclusion of an item for profit. That only applies to Prime Cost Sums for nominated subcontractors and nominated suppliers.

▶ The BoQ description for facing bricks defines the bricks as 'pc £X per 1,000'. What is included in this pc sum?

The bricks themselves constitute a 'defined provisional sum' as defined in General Rule 10 and the pc sum is to be treated as a defined provisional sum for the supply of facing bricks.

General Rule 10.3 describes what constitutes a defined provisional sum. General Rule 10.4 states what the contractor has deemed to include in the price. This includes an allowance for programming, planning and pricing preliminaries.

The architect will issue an architect's instruction omitting the prime cost of the bricks and will add back a specific type of brick at a specific cost. This cost will be calculated by taking account of the actual cost of the bricks delivered to the site plus normal profit and overheads and be substituted for the provisional cost. The remainder of the rate build up will remain unchanged because the labour cost and the costs of other materials, fixing in position, plant, waste, square cutting, establishment, overhead charges and profit are deemed included within the rest of the Bill rate as required by General Rule 4.6.

# 11  Work not covered

▶ The tender documents state 'preparation drawings are to be provided by the contractor'. How is this requirement measured?

It is measured in a similar manner to the measurement rules of Work Sections R, X and Y, namely R10.16, X.17, Y51.6 and Y81.7.

# 13  Work to existing buildings

▶ A BoQ contains an item for installing new electrical wiring below an existing timber floor. There is a qualification to the SMM7 rules in the preamble stating 'lifting floor boards and removing ceilings, etc. and all subsequent making good is deemed included within the items of rewiring'. Can two items of work that normally should be measured separately under the rules of SMM7 be lumped together in one Bill item if the preamble to the Bill contains the relevant qualification?

Yes, it has always been held that any of the rules of SMM7 can be amended, adapted, amalgamated, omitted, etc. provided the specific departures from the rules of SMM7 are clearly stated somewhere within the tender document.

# A Preliminaries/General conditions

▶ Must items in the preliminaries section of the Bill of quantities be valued only by the percentage of work carried out?

No, Definition Rules A.D1 and A.D2 define which items or parts of items in the preliminaries are to be valued as 'fixed' or 'time' related. Clause 3.2 on page 7 of the *Measurement Code* also describes how preliminary items are to be split.

## A35 Employer's requirements: Specific limitations on method/sequence/timing/use of site

▶ The specification states that the PVC windows are to be set into preformed openings in the brick walls. To form these openings the contractor must construct templates. Should these templates be measured?

No, they are temporary items and therefore not measurable. The specification requirement is a limitation on the contractor's method of working therefore must be mentioned in the Preliminaries in accordance with A35.1.2. This allows the contractor the opportunity of pricing for the templates.

## A51 Nominated subcontractors

▶ Please define the payment of nominated subcontractors' overhead charges.

General Rule 4.6 qualifies the list of items deemed included with the words 'Unless otherwise specifically stated in a BoQ or herein'. The term 'overhead charges' used in General Rule 4.6(g) refers to all overheads whether charged to site or head office.

▶ Is the main contractor's % profit on a pc sum a fixed lump sum?

No, it is a % and the amount will vary with the Nominated Subcontract value.

▶ Please define special attendance?

Special attendance comprises one or more of the items listed in A51.1.3.1–8 and clarified by Definition Rules A51.D8 and D9.

▶ What is meant by positioning as referred to in A51.1.3.4?

Definition Rule A51.D9 defines special attendance of 'Positioning'. Unloading heavy items of plant would comply with this definition and should be measured as such.

# A53  Work by statutory authorities

▶ Is the main contractor entitled to overheads and profit on the expenditure of an undefined provisional sum for 'Work by statutory authorities'?

Yes.

# C Existing site/buildings/services

## Important note

All references now relate to SMM7 revised 1998, incorporating amendments 1 and 2 (2000). Work Section C was renumbered, some items were combined and some new sections were created.

## C20 Demolition

## C21 Toxic/Hazardous material removal

## C30 Shoring/Facade retention

▶ A BoQ description for demolition of a building describes the building and refers to a drawing. It states that the building be demolished down to 'existing ground level'. The preamble states that 'a set of original construction drawings' is available for inspection. The structure included a substantial reinforced concrete undercroft [a semi-cellar or void, partly below ground, not full height] below the suspended ground floor but above the external ground level. Should the demolition of this undercroft be considered as an 'Extra'?

No, the BoQ item complies with C20.1.1.1. It accurately describes the level down to which the structure must be demolished.

We were instructed to remove skirtings and make good with plaster. Does this include repairs to wall plaster above skirting level and the provision of new skirtings?

No, the making good of the wall plaster would only apply to the specific area of wall finish affected by removal of skirtings. It would not include a new skirting.

The BoQ includes an item to demolish a wall 400mm thick, part of the wall is 700mm thick, is the extra thickness remeasurable?

The removal of the 700mm thick wall is subject to remeasurement in accordance with C20.2.1.

▶ Included in a BoQ item for the demolition of a structure are items for the disconnection of gas and electric services and their subsequent removal. Are these deemed to be included under clause C20.1.1.1.5?

The temporary disconnection of gas and electric services is deemed included in SMM7 measurement item C20.1.1.1.5. Any permanent work to these supplies such as permanent disconnection or sealing off should be measured separately, either as a provisional sum under Section A53 or as measured items within the Mechanical and electrical works.

The removal of meters prior to demolition should be measured in accordance with C90.2.1.

# SMM7 Q & A

Is the removal of furniture and other loose items deemed included in the demolition item of a building measured in accordance with C20.1?

No, their removal should be measured separately.

How should the removal of the following items, which must be executed prior to demolition, be measured?

Fridges

Furniture

Sanitary items

Carpets

The removal of fixtures, fittings and carpets prior to demolition would be measured separately as follows:

**Fridges** – C90.1.1.*.4 (special conditions apply to the disposal of refrigerators – the coolant in old fridges is toxic).

**Furniture** – C90.1.1.

**Sanitary items** – C90.2.1.

**Carpets** – C90.3.1 or 4.1 (depending on whether the carpet was laid loose or stuck down with adhesive).

Should the specific type of asbestos be given in a Bill description for its removal?

If known, yes, otherwise a provisional item should be given.

An existing building is to be partially demolished. The item of work concerns the temporary support of parts of an existing staircase that is to be retained, whilst adjoining elements of the staircase structure are demolished. The parts of the staircase that are to be demolished consist of two of its surrounding walls, with the remaining walls being retained along with the stairs themselves.

New construction work then abuts the existing staircase. Once this new work is complete, the existing structure is integral with the new works and is, in itself, structurally sound.

However, until such times as the new works have been completed, temporary propping and bracing is required to be installed to maintain structural integrity of the remaining staircase walls and stairs.

Are the temporary propping and bracing works for the retained elements of the staircase required to be separately identified in the Bills, measurable as an item in accordance with item C20.4 of the Classification Table 'Support of structures not to be demolished', or would the temporary support work properly fall under a measured item in accordance with item C20.3 of the Classification Table 'Demolishing parts of structures'?

Any shoring that is not at the discretion of the contractor and is required to temporarily support structures not being demolished must be measured in accordance with C20.4.1.*.1–6 and defined in Definition Rule C20.D4.

All other incidental shoring or support work that is solely at the discretion of the contractor is deemed included within C20.1–3 as stated in Coverage Rule C20.C1(b).

> The front and rear façade panels of a terrace house are to be removed leaving the roof intact. The drawings indicate and specify that temporary shoring must be erected to support the roof. Is this temporary support work measurable or is it deemed to be incidental to the demolition work?

As the decision to erect the shoring is not left to the discretion of the contractor it must be measured in accordance with C20.4.1.*.1–6.

# C40 Cleaning masonry/concrete

# C41 Repairing/Renovating/Conserving masonry

# C42 Repairing/Renovating/Conserving concrete

> Should the description for 'raking out and repointing joints of existing brickwork' include specific reference to the hardness of the existing mortar? The tender documents state that the tenderers must ascertain for themselves, by inspection, the nature and complexity of the works.

No, provided the Bill item has included all information regarding the extent and location of the work the onus lies with the contractor to visit the site of the proposed works to ascertain matters such as the hardness of mortar.

> A Bill item has been measured for a new expansion joint to be inserted into an existing brick wall. No mention is made in the item for cutting out the brickwork to receive this joint. Is the cutting and subsequent making good of the brickwork deemed included in the item for the expansion joint?

No, General Rule 4.2 does not allow the aggregation of a number of items which are otherwise required to be measured separately. The cutting of the brickwork should be measured in accordance with C40.3.

> Cleaning areas of concrete have been measured to ceilings, walls and columns. The various surfaces are both below and over 300mm wide. Should the areas less than 300mm wide be measured in linear metres?

No, all areas are added together and given in $m^2$ as C40.6.1.

> Concrete repairs in isolated areas are generally measured in depth ranges and surface areas enumerated. In the instance where a repair has to be cut back and repaired to three differing depths, do you take an average over the three areas and measure as one overall repair or do you measure each one in its respective band and measure as three repairs?

The measurement of concrete repairs can be measured either in $m^2$, linear metres or be enumerated in accordance with C42.1.1.1–3. Separate items must be measured for areas with different depths.

> Should the repointing of different types of brickwork and a multi-course slate DPC band, all within one wall elevation, be measured as separate items?

Separate items should be measured for the repointing of each type of facing brick and the slate damp course, C41.4.1.1.1 and Measurement Rule C41.M2.

There is an item in the BoQ for repointing brickwork. The Bill item comprises only one area in m² whereas the actual circumstances are numerous small isolated areas each less than 1m² – is this Bill item sufficient to describe the exact circumstances?

The description should differentiate between large areas and numerous small isolated areas. General Rule 1.1 requires the surveyor to give more detailed information than is required by the rules in order to define the precise nature and extent of the required work.

In calculating the area of precast concrete wall panels to be cleaned by pressure jet washing the surveyor has calculated the area of a single panel and then multiplied that area by the number of panels. This does not take account of the area taken up by the 12mm wide joints. How should the area to be cleaned be measured?

The area measured should be the overall length by height of the wall including the area of joints.

# C90 Alterations – spot items

Does a Bill item for the removal of a sheet vinyl floor include the removal of the entire adhesive bed from the subfloor base?

In the absence of any specific information it is left to the discretion of the contractor to leave the subfloor in a condition suitable to receive the new finish as specified.

A Bill item describes the removing of a floor finish complete with its screed. Should a separate item be measured for removing floor finishes that do not have a screed below them?

Yes, if some areas of floor finish are not laid on a screed, the work being described differs.

Does a Bill description for removing vinyl flooring back to the screed infer that there may be more than one layer of vinyl flooring?

No, if multiple layers are subsequently encountered, the work of removing the floor is sufficiently different from what the BoQ description inferred that it should be remeasured as executed.

Should a BoQ item for patching small areas of plaster in repairs assume the removal of wallpaper as part of the preparation to plastering?

No, removal of wallpaper should be measured separately, either as C90.3 or Additional Rules – work to existing buildings, item 2 (page 171 of SMM7).

# D Groundwork

## D20 Excavating and filling

## Q20 Granular sub-bases to roads/pavings

▶ How is dewatering of a localised area of excavation work measured if:
  (a) the water has collected in the excavations from broken field drains;
  (b) the excavations encounter non-recorded ground water?

It is measured as:

(a) Disposal of surface water, D20.8.1;
(b) Disposal of ground water, D20.8.2 from the recorded depth as encountered.

▶ Does this still apply if the tender document allowed for work below ground water level and the only difference is that the post contract ground water level is 1000mm higher?

Measurement Rule D20.M5 states that if the post contract water level differs from the pre-contract water level the measurements are revised accordingly.

▶ Does temporary pumping of water from land drains and sumps fall under 'Site Dewatering' for which there are no specific rules of measurement.

No, pumping water from land drain sumps and their associated pipework would be measured as disposal of surface water in accordance with D20.8.1, Measurement Rule D20.M12 and Definition Rule D20.11.

▶ Must 'working space allowance to excavations' be allowed for, regardless of depth or width of trench?

Working space must be measured in accordance with D20.6 and Measurement Rule D20.M7 and is measured irrespective of width or depth of trench.

▶ How does the SMM7 deal with the disposal of contaminated spoil?

See D20.8.3.1.1– 4.

▶ If the tender documents make a specific demand on where excavated topsoil is to be stockpiled should this requirement be mentioned in the Bill description?

Yes, the stockpiling would be measured in accordance with D20.8.3.2.1 and 2.

Further explanation can be found on page 19 of the *Measurement Code*, in item 8.3.

▶ Imported filling to excavation has been measured in accordance with D20.9.1–2.3. Measurement Rule D20.M14 states 'Filling is measured as equal to the void filled'. Does this mean the actual void excavated or the theoretical void to be filled?

The term 'equal to the void filled' as used in M14 means the void excavated in accordance with the information or instructions. Any over excavation must be filled at the contractor's own expense.

▶ A ground beam trench is lined with a compressible liner to retain the concrete. Should this liner be measured as formwork therefore requiring the measurement of working space allowance to excavations?

No, the liner is not capable of supporting the weight of concrete therefore can not be classed as formwork.

If this method of construction was designed by the structural engineer the method of construction is not at the discretion of the contractor and details must be given in Preliminaries Section A35.1.1.

▶ The contractor's chosen method of fabricating long lengths of ground beam reinforcement is in the excavated trench. Does this mean that the surveyor must include working space allowance to excavations when remeasuring the earthworks?

No, the method and location of fabricating reinforcement is left to the discretion of the contractor.

▶ Should the level of ground water given in the tender documents anticipate the time of year when the excavations are likely to be carried out?

The ground water level provided in the tender documents should be a reasonable indication of what is likely to be expected. The level will be established from trial holes and will be given in accordance with the relevant British Standard Code of Practice.

Should the post contract ground water level be the average mean level over the entire period that excavations are executed and left open?

The post contract ground water level will be established at the time each excavation is carried out, D20.P1(b).

It is not intended that several water levels, with only minor variations, be established for each location of excavation. Clause P1 on page 18 of the *Measurement Code* gives further clarification. In most cases it should be possible to agree a common post contract ground water level for the whole of the site.

Should 'working space allowance' be made when sheet piling has been used?

No.

▶ The specification for hardcore fill states that bulk fill must be laid in layers not exceeding 250mm thick. The finished thickness of the fill is 1250mm. Should compacting to the filling be measured for each 250mm thick layer of fill or only once to the total finished thickness of fill?

Once, after all of the layers have been laid. The item of compacting relates to the measurement of the surface treatment, D20.13.2.2.

How is 'work below ground water level' remeasured when no 'post contract ground water level' was established because the contractor chose to construct foundations in short lengths using the trench fill technique?

Using actual measured depths or other agreed records, an average post contract ground water level for the site can be calculated.

Should interlocking sheet steel piling earthwork support be measured if it has not been designed and specified?

No, see Definition Rule D20.D7.

▶ Should an 'extra over any type of excavation' item be measured for excavating 'non-hazardous industrial waste'.

Only if the contractor had to take specific special precautions when carrying out the excavations, Measurement Rule D20.M6.

Please explain the measurement of disposal of contaminated excavated material.

The disposal of excavated material is measured in accordance with D20.8.3.1.1–4. Separate items must be measured for each and every type of contaminated material and the different method of disposal or location of disposal.

▶ Should earthwork support be measured even if not used and the sides of the excavation stepped?

Yes, see D20.7, Measurement Rule M9.

▶ How should the disposal of ground water be measured if the water is contaminated?

Provided the tender documents inform tenderers that ground water is contaminated, the disposal is at the discretion of the contractor, subject to the contractor complying with all relevant current statutory regulations and to any limitations or restrictions contained within the tender documents.

▶ What constitutes 'special plant' as referred to in the description of breaking out rock, etc?

Examples of special plant are contained in D5 on page 19 of the *Measurement Code*. These examples include items such as power operated hammers, drills and chisels, and special attachments to mechanical plant such as rock buckets, rippers, hammers and chisels. This list is not exhaustive.

▶ Where an item for excavating pits for round manholes has been measured, does Coverage Rule D20.C3 mean the contractor must allow in the rates for:
- additional excavation in digging a square pit (it not being practical to machine dig a round pit)?

Yes.

- additional concrete surround?

Yes.

▶ Is working space allowance a measurable item for manholes 4m deep?

It is allowable only if the requirements of Definition Rule D20.M7 occur. The depth of excavation in itself is not a reason to measure a working space allowance item.

▶ Should there be an item measured for temporary disposal on site of topsoil prior to subsequent re-use?

Yes, if the retention or disposal of topsoil on site is not left to the discretion of the contractor.

▶ Please define the measurement of compaction to different types of filling and blinding.

Compacting surfaces of fill must be measured for each type of fill measured, D20.13.2.2.

Each specific blinding bed must be measured as filling, D20.M18, and therefore an item for compacting surface of this blinding bed must also be measured.

▶ Should earthwork support to unstable ground be measured separately from areas of general earthwork support?

Yes, see D20.7.1–3.1–3.3. The quantities of 'earthwork to unstable ground' will be subject to remeasurement upon completion of work, thus reflecting actual ground conditions encountered during excavations.

▶ The ground in the excavations is unstable. Must the QS measure interlocking sheet piling?

No, earthwork support extending into unstable ground must be so described D20.1.1–3.1–3.3.

Interlocking sheet steel piling can only be measured if its use is not left to the discretion of the contractor.

▶ Bill items for excavation commencing at specified levels below existing ground level are described as 'provisional'. Would these items be considered to be 'defined' or 'undefined' provisional works?

The excavation items referred to comply with General Rule 10.3 in that they provide all necessary information considered to be 'defined work' and therefore all due allowances referred to in General Rule 10.4 would be deemed included in the Contract Sum.

▶ Land drains are severed during the course of trench excavation and partially flood the trenches. Can the de-watering be classed as 'Disposal of ground water'?

No, disposal of water appearing in excavations as a result of severed land drains is 'Disposal of surface water', Definition Rule D20.D11.

Disposal of ground water can only be measured if excavations are deeper than the specified level of the ground water, Measurement Rule D20.M12.

▶ Working space allowance has been measured to all four sides of a manhole pit. Should deductions be made for the open ends of outgoing pipe trenches?

The working space allowance would be measured across outgoing trench ends because the area is related to the area of formwork, Measurement Rule D20.M8.

▶ When measuring earthwork support to the sides of a manhole pit should deductions be made for the open ends of outgoing pipe trenches?

Earthwork support would not be measured across open ends of outgoing pipe trenches. There is no face to support, Measurement Rule D20.M9.

The excavation quantities for a swimming pool, a basement tank room and a pond have all been lumped under one heading of 'Excavating to reduce level'. Is this correct?

No, the excavation work to the swimming pool and basement tank room should be described as 'Excavating basements and the like', D20.2.3.

The pond excavation would be described as 'reduced level excavation', D20.2.2. It would not be incorrect to provide additional information to the item explaining that the reduce level excavation is to create a pond.

The edges of the concrete path require formwork. What is the area of 'working space allowance'?

The area of working space allowance is calculated by multiplying the girth of formwork, rendering, tanking or protective walls by the depth of excavation below commencing level of excavation, Measurement Rule D20.M8.

The depth would be that indicated by dimension A in the sketch below.

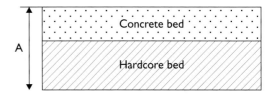

How is the work involved in breaking out obstructions below reduce level excavation measured?

It is measured by calculating the volume of the obstruction in accordance with the rules of Work Section D20.4. These quantities can then be priced at Bill rates, pro rata or fair rates.

If the obstruction is encountered during piling operations then item D30.5.1 would apply and time would be recorded.

What superficial items of treatment must be measured when earth mounds are to be formed from excavated material obtained from on-site spoil heaps and covered with topsoil also obtained from on-site spoil heaps. The sides of the mounds are formed to gradients both below and above 15 degrees?

Items required to be measured to surfaces of formed mounds are:
- D20.12.1 – this item would only apply to surfaces which are $> 15°$ from horizontal.
- D20.13.2.2 – this item would only apply to surfaces which are $\leq 15°$ from horizontal.
- D20.13.5 – this item will be measured to all surfaces of mounds irrespective of slope.

What is the demarcation between 'Excavate to reduce levels' and 'Excavate basements and the like'?

'Reduce level excavation' would be all excavation necessary to reduce the level of ground down to a specified formation level from which other types of excavation, such as basement excavations, would commence.

▶ If ground levels are reduced to a specified level and then a cut, say 10m wide x 1m deep, is made for a road sub-base, would that cut excavation be classed as 'basement excavation' or some other type of excavation other than 'reduce level'?

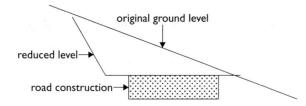

No, it would still be considered to be 'excavation to reduce levels' but different items of 'reduce level excavation' must be measured for different depth ranges and differing commencing levels, D20 2.2.1–4.1.

'Excavating basements or the like' would be usually only be measured when excavating below a general formation level to create a basement below a building.

▶ Must breaking up of hard surface pavings be measured as 'Extra over any type of excavation irrespective or depth' or can it be measured on its own?

This work can be measured either as full value in m², D20.5.*.1–5.1 or as extra over in m², D20.5.2.5.1.

As the extra over option is in the fourth column of the Classification Table the choice is optional, see General Rule 2.6.

▶ Please clarify how the measurement of the 'working space allowance for formwork' is calculated.

The area of working space allowance is calculated by multiplying the girth of the formwork by the depth of the excavation below the commencing level of excavation, provided the face of the excavation is less than 600mm from the face of the formwork, rendering, tanking or protective walls. See Measurement Rules D20.M7 and M8.

In the case of formwork being 100mm thick blockwork, the girth is taken as the inner face of the blockwork in contact with the face of the concrete.

▶ Should a Bill item of 'Extra over any type of excavation, breaking up limestone' be measured and paid for if 'special means' as described in Definition Rule D20.D5 are not needed to break up and remove the limestone?

Yes, by describing the material as limestone it is left to the discretion of the contractor as to how it is broken up.

▶ A BoQ item is measured for 'clearing site vegetation'. Does this item include the excavation of topsoil?

No.

▶ Structural drawings provide for two alternative methods of constructing a retaining wall. The BoQ measured one method, i.e. excavating back to a vertical face and supporting the earthwork with trench sheeting. The contractor carried out the work by the other method, i.e. excavating to a batter and therefore having to backfill a greater volume and reinstate a larger surface area. Should the work be remeasured as executed?

Yes, where the method of carrying out the work is left to the discretion of the contractor, work shall be remeasured as executed.

▶ Does a Bill item for 'disposal of excavated material off site' include the loading of the excavated material into the lorry?

Yes, the method of disposing excavated material is left to the discretion of the contractor. The contractor can either load the material directly into lorries or deposit it in temporary spoil heaps on site to be loaded and removed off site later.

▶ During excavation works the contractor encountered conditions described by the structural engineer as 'backfill over completely weathered to highly weathered sandstone'. The structural engineer states that this material would not require any special excavation techniques or plant to remove the sandstone. The contractor is claiming an 'extra over' item for breaking up the sandstone because he had to use a pecker and compressor. Is he entitled to this?

Yes, a pecker would be similar to a chisel and therefore considered to be 'special plant' as defined in Definition Rule D20.D5 and on page 19 of the *Measurement Code*.

▶ Billed rock quantities are 80m³ and actual excavated quantities are 2300m³. Only one item for breaking out rock has been given but only on the basis of 80m³ being excavated. If 2300m³ had been evident at billing stage, should the QS have given separate break out items against each element, i.e. breaking out rock in trenches, in pits, etc?

No.

'Extra over' item D20.4.*.1 for breaking out rock is intended to cover 'any type of excavation irrespective of depth'. There is no specific requirement within the rules for separate quantities of rock breaking to be measured for each type of excavation listed under D20.2.2–8.

▶ If a contractor excavates a foundation pit to the exact size of a foundation base and pours the in situ concrete directly into the pit, should the following items be measured:
  • earthwork support?
  • working space allowance?
  • formwork to the concrete?

  • Yes, see D20.M9.
  • No, see D20.M7.
  • No, the concrete must be described as 'poured on or against earth or unblended hardcore'.

▶ Must concrete blinding to the bottom of a foundation be measured if not shown on drawings or specified?

No.

▶ Should an item of 'surface treatment', in the form of compacting, be measured to a 25mm thick bed of sand blinding (measured in m³ in accordance with D20.10) which includes 'compacting' within its description?

Yes.

▶ A Bill item for 'Hardcore, crusher run stone; broken to 65mm maximum gauge' makes no reference to where this fill is to be obtained.

Can the contractor assume 'materials arising from the excavations'?

No.

# SMM7 Q & A

Must an item of 'surface treatments to ground or bottoms of excavations' be measured for all excavated areas?

No, only if specified or instructed.

A BoQ item is measured full value for 'Breaking up 150mm reinforced concrete road including 300mm sub-base, dispose off site'. Does this item also include the reduce level excavation and disposal?

No, the reduce level and disposal measurements will commence from the exposed surface after removal of the road and sub-base.

See the sketch below.

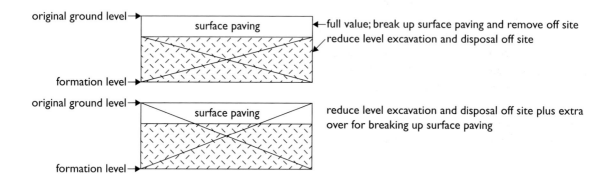

A contractor deliberately excavated stanchion bases to larger dimensions than shown on the drawings and cast the concrete directly into the pits.

Are items for formwork and working space measurable in lieu of the additional concrete?

Formwork and working space will not be measured but the concrete in the stanchion bases will be measured to the sizes shown on the drawings and described as 'poured on or against earth unblinded hardcore' in accordance with E10.1 or 3.*.*.1 and 5. This would allow the rate for the concrete to be adjusted for the 'waste concrete' that would arise from pouring the concrete against the earth.

The specification requires that concrete ground beams be cast directly into their trenches using a proprietary semi-rigid liner to line the sides of the trenches as a 'permanent' formwork. Should this liner be classed as formwork thereby requiring that the 'working space allowance' be measured in the excavation section?

No, the liner material is not capable of supporting the weight of the concrete unaided. It is a separating membrane and should be measured as such.

The 'working space allowance' should not be measured.

Excavations were carried out in old filled ground for a new road. The exposed surface was graded, levelled and rolled prior to soil stabilisation. Is a Bill item for 'trimming' required before stabilisation work starts?

An item for 'compacting' the reduced level work surface should be measured in accordance with D20.13.2.3. Trimming refers only to vertical or sloping sides of excavation.

Items for earthwork support were also measured to the vertical sides of the excavation, is a Bill item also required for 'working space'?

Working space allowance is only measured if formwork, rendering, tanking or protective walls occur, as described in Measurement Rules D20.M7 and M8.

▶ Imagine if you will a football pitch with a basement excavation at the centre circle. Piling was carried out from a piling mat at pitch level and whilst piles were required to the underside of the basement base, they were installed from pitch level and subsequently broken down in the basement area. This obviously necessitated careful excavation around the piles for the basement excavation and accordingly an extra over rate was submitted.

The work is however remeasured on completion so this 'temporary state' is not reflected on the drawings, it being the principal contractors chosen method of working unadvised at tender. The SMM7 make no reference for works of this nature other than a reference at D20.7 for ground beams. The principal contractor is reluctant to make payment as there is no item measurable by SMM7.

The extra 'work' involved in excavating around piles would be considered a special requirement as referred to in Supplementary Information item D20.S2. The work would be measured (or remeasured) as 'extra over any type of excavation irrespective of depth for excavating around piles' in accordance with D20.3 and enumerated.

▶ Should earthwork support or working space be measured if interlocking driven sheet piles are put in place prior to excavations commencing?

No.

▶ Must the breaking up of surface paving be measured separately from the reduce level excavation items?

Breaking up of surface pavings can be measured either full value in m² as D20.5.*.1–5 or as 'extra over' the relevant excavation item as D20.5.*.1–5.1. The reference to 'extra over' in the 4th column of the SMM7 is to provide an **option** to measuring full value. How disposal of the spoil from the surface pavings is measured will depend on whether the breaking up has been measured full value or extra over.

The total volume of material excavated must be included in the disposal items. If the breaking up of the surface paving has been measured 'full value' then the volume of the surface paving must be added to the volume of material to be disposed.

▶ SMM7 states under D20 (Excavating and filling) and R12 (Drainage below ground) 'commencing level stated where exceeding 0.25m below existing ground level'. In the absence of this being stated should the measurement of excavations commence from ground level?

In the absence of any commencing level being given in a Bill description of excavation, it would be correct to assume that the commencement level was existing ground level.

▶ We have unreinforced concrete pad foundations described as poured on against earth. We have measured earthwork support but not formwork and not working space. The subcontractor has completed phase 1 of the project without using formwork and he did not apply for formwork or working space in the final account.

However prior to starting phase 2 the subcontractor has stated that either he is paid for working space (even if formwork is not used) or he intends to use formwork and apply for the cost of formwork and working space. Are there any situations other than those described in D20.M7 under which working space could be measured to pad foundations?

If the concrete is poured directly into the ground the concrete must be so described, E10.1.*.*.5, and the rate for the concrete shall allow for over-pour wastage. Neither formwork nor working space shall be measured.

No.

There are no situations other than described in D20.M7 that would entitle working space to be measured.

▶ We had been instructed under the contract to strip the topsoil in the car park areas, place engineered fill in layers from reduced level up to the underside of an MOT type 1 stone layer detailed as 325mm thick, with final levels being given on the drawing for the macadam surfacing.

This scenario is similar to the first, with the work indicated to the roads. In this instance there are again two layers of material. The first being a capping layer over the reduced level dig, detailed as 150mm thick of 6F1 stone and the second being a 250mm thick layer of MOT type 1 stone up to the underside of the macadam.

Due to there being two distinct materials each with levels and thicknesses indicated on the drawings are we entitled to measure an item for level and compact to both layers of fill material in each scenario?

Yes, an item of 'compacting surfaces of filling' must be measured for each and every type of fill material laid.

# D30 Piling

▶ **Cast in place concrete piling** – How should earthwork support between contiguous piles be measured in the BoQ:
- where soil retained is shown from soil reports as being stable?
- where soil retained is shown as being unstable?

Contiguous piling should mean that there is no gap between piles. However, if there is a gap then the usual items for the measurement of earthwork support contained in Work Section D20 should be followed and adapted to suit this specific situation.

# D50 Underpinning

▶ Is the temporary support referred to in D50.1 a risk item?

No, temporary support for existing structures, D50.1, is not a 'risk item'. If it was not provided, it cannot be measured.

Is the measurement of width allowances for underpinning preliminary trenches and underpinning pits adjustable?

Width allowances are not adjustable and should be allowed whether more or less has been used. Allowances are left to the discretion of the contractor.

Do the maximum depth stages for preliminary trenches and underpinning pits refer to the combined depths of trench and pit or are they each considered separately?

Maximum depth stages for preliminary trenches and underpinning pits should be considered separately.

▶ Should working space allowance be measured in underpinning excavations?

Working space for formwork in underpinning excavations is not measured. The width allowances that must be applied to the preliminary trench excavation and under-pinning pits (D50.M1(a), (b) and (c)) provide the necessary working space to place the formwork.

▶ Please advise on your interpretation of the measurement for width allowances as stipulated in the underpinning section D50 of SMM7.

Measurement Rules D50.M1, M2 and M3 of SMM7 describe how the widths of preliminary trenches and underpinning pits are calculated.

In all cases, the 'width allowance' **must** be added to the width of the projection of any existing foundation to be retained plus the width of any projection of the underpinning. In all cases, the width of projections is calculated from the face of the existing wall. These minimum widths must be measured whether or not required.

# E  In situ concrete/Large precast concrete

## E05  In situ concrete construction generally

## E10  Mixing/Casting/Curing in situ concrete

▶ What is the distinction between E05 and E10?

Both are to be read together:
- E05 refers to general concrete construction;
- E10 refers to the placing, compacting and curing of all types of concrete mixes, strengths and workmanship to a particular project.

See CAWS for a more detailed explanation.

▶ A contractor deliberately excavated stanchion bases to larger dimensions than shown on the drawings and cast the concrete directly into the pits.

Are items for formwork and working space measurable in lieu of the additional concrete?

Formwork and working space will not be measured but the concrete in the stanchion bases will be measured to the sizes shown on the drawings and described as 'poured on or against earth unblinded hardcore' in accordance with E10.1 or 3.*.*.1 and 5. This would allow the rate for the concrete to be adjusted for the 'waste concrete' that would arise from pouring the concrete against the earth.

Please define the measurement of a concrete slab on metal formwork.

There is no need to make reference to metal decking when measuring a concrete slab on metal deck formwork.

The volume of concrete measured should be the exact volume, therefore voids created by ribs should be omitted.

How is the concrete in margins in troughed slabs measured?

The concrete in margins that are ≤ 500mm wide is included in the item for troughed slabs, Definition Rule E10.D5. If the margin exceeds 500mm wide the concrete is measured as ordinary slabs.

Should concrete in a column base be described as reinforced if the only reinforcement is starter bars?

Yes, if the bars have to be set in position before the concrete is poured.

Should 'grouting stanchion bases' be deemed included in a 'contractor designed' structural steel package?

Not if the tender documentation does not specify it. The work should be measured in E10.16.1.

Is there any need to identify structural members that are fully embedded within a concrete wall?

There is no need to refer to a structural steel member embedded within an in situ concrete wall.

The relationship between structural steel members and other parts of the building must be shown on drawings that must be provided in accordance with Information Rule G10.P1(a).

How is the concrete in attached column casings measured?

Columns and column casings are only measured when isolated, Measurement Rule E40.M4.

How are concrete walls containing cross bracing measured?

Concrete is measured as a wall where the cross bracing is located within the thickness of the wall.

▶ Should the concrete to a manhole base that is reinforced with mesh be described as 'reinforced'?

Yes.

If so, must formwork be measured?

Only if specified.

If formwork is specified must 'working space' be measured?

Yes.

Should formwork be measured when concrete is described as poured against earth/hardcore?

No.

▶ Please define the measurement of concrete to a hollow rib decking.

Measurement Rule E10.M1 states 'concrete volume is measured net'. The volume of the ribs of the hollow rib decking would be deducted from the overall quantity.

# E20  Formwork for in situ concrete

▶ The specification requires that concrete ground beams be cast directly into their trenches using a proprietary semi-rigid liner to line the sides of the trenches as a 'permanent' formwork. Should this liner be classed as formwork thereby requiring that the 'working space allowance' be measured in the excavation section?

No, the liner material is not capable of supporting the weight of the concrete unaided. It is a separating membrane and should be measured as such.

The 'working space allowance' should not be measured.

Is curved formwork measurable to circular concrete surrounds to precast concrete manhole rings?

Curved formwork to concrete surround and working space should be measured if specified. If concrete has been poured against the sides of a pit then the item for concrete should be so described thereby allowing the estimator the opportunity of allowing for waste concrete in the rate.

▶ Is it permissible for a specification to state 'strike formwork without disturbing props'?

Yes, this becomes a method and sequence of work not at the discretion of the contractor therefore must be referred to in Section A35 of the preliminaries.

▶ If the permissible loadings that formwork must be capable of supporting are not given in the tender documents, is it correct for the contractor to assume that the height of formwork from soffits is calculated down to the highest point above ground level capable of supporting the load?

Yes.

If the top surface of an in situ slab is specified to finish with a camber should the formwork be described as 'curved'?

Only if the soffit is specified to finish with a curve.

Must formwork be measured to in situ concrete ground beams?

Yes, unless the specification states otherwise, Coverage Rule E10.C1.

▶ Should 'through propping' be measured if a slab is incapable of supporting the weight of formwork and concrete being constructed on the floor above it?

Yes, the soffit height is related to the highest point capable of supporting the load, therefore, if a slab is not able to support the formwork and concrete of the slab above it, then the soffit height must be taken from the lowest slab capable of supporting the weight. If through propping is needed, this must be indicated in the formwork description.

Where vertical surfaces to columns are over 3.5m high, should a separate item be measured?

Yes, as E20.15–16.1–2.*.1

Should formwork to parapet walls be measured as 'walls' or 'upstand beams'?

It should be measured as formwork to walls in accordance with E20.12.

Should trough length of formwork to soffits of troughed slabs be given in the description?

No.

Are the soffits of ribs over 500mm wide which border panels of troughed slab separate surfaces?

Yes.

When measuring formwork to pile caps, what deductions are made for attached ground beams?

No deductions are made for passings, as stated in Measurement Rule E20.M3.

▶ What item(s) of formwork should be measured to the edge of ground beams and edges of beds that contain a rebate (see sketch below).

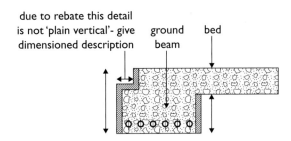

due to rebate this detail is not 'plain vertical'- give dimensioned description | ground beam | bed

The formwork can be measured in one of two ways depending on the order of placing the concrete. The surveyor should state which order has been assumed in the Bill description.

- If the ground beam is cast in one operation – one linear item of formwork with reference to a dimensioned description as E20.2.2 plus an item for forming rebate, E20.19.1.

- If the ground beam is cast in two operations – two linear items of plain formwork as E20.2.2.

▶ A reinforced concrete wall is constructed with several structural steel columns and beams encased within the concrete. There are no projections on the wall faces. Should the formwork to those faces of the wall that contain the steel sections be measured as beam and column casings?

No, the formwork should be measured as 'to walls' leaving the method of pouring and construction to the discretion of the contractor. Rule G10.P1 states that drawings must be provided to show the relative position of the steelwork to other parts of the work and the proposed building.

▶ Circumstances on site dictated that blinding concrete be poured into part of a trench in order to form a vertical face for the strip foundation to be cast against. This blinding concrete needed formwork to only one face. Should this type of formwork be described separately from other types of foundation formwork?

Yes, see detail below.

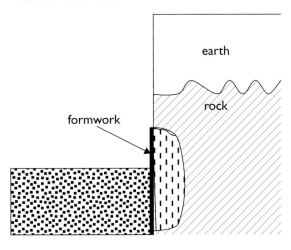

earth

rock

formwork

▶ A concrete floor slab is laid after the outer wall is built. Should the blockwork be measured as 'permanent formwork'?

No.

How is formwork to the soffit and edge of a suspended slab measured where:

- the 'suspended slab' is laid on compacted hardcore?
- the edge abuts a brick wall that may be constructed before or after the slab is poured?

Formwork is only measured to surfaces of concrete which require to be supported, Measurement Rule E20.M1.

- No formwork is measured if the hardcore can carry the weight of the concrete.
- The order of works is left to the discretion of the contractor. Formwork should not be measured if the wall is able to support the edge of the bed. If formwork is required, it should be measured as edges of beds, E20.2.1.3.

How should formwork be described when being measured to 500 × 100mm reinforced concrete columns that are integral with a reinforced concrete wall but project from the face?

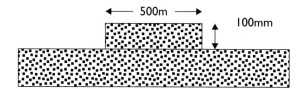

It should be described as formwork to walls, because the length on plan is greater than four times the thickness of the attached column.

If an in situ concrete wall is constructed in a different order from that assumed by the QS when measuring the formwork for the BoQ, should the formwork be measured as executed?

Yes.

The original Bills of approximate quantities for the substructure were measured in accordance with SMM7. Items and quantities were based upon an incomplete design, the tender was based upon the BoQ, no design drawings were provided. If foundation concrete is not described as 'poured on or against earth or unblinded concrete' should formwork be measured to sides of foundations?

Yes.

Once on site the foundations were cast into formwork. Must the formwork be remeasured?

Yes, executed work is remeasured in accordance with rules relevant to whichever work section is being remeasured. If concrete is cast against earth it is remeasured as such. If formwork is used it would be remeasured.

Foundation bases were dug neat to the actual size required. The reinforcement was prefabricated and subsequently lowered in position. The concrete was then placed against the face of excavation as there was no requirement to provide formwork.

Should formwork be measured to the sides of the concrete bases and in turn an entitlement to measure working space?

Executed work is remeasured in accordance with rules relevant to whichever work section is being remeasured. If concrete is cast against earth it is remeasured as such. Formwork cannot be remeasured if not provided.

# SMM7 Q & A

A reinforced concrete wall is cast with openings left out from the top edge to facilitate the construction of dock-loaders. These openings measure 3 x 1.5m. Should their area be deducted when calculating the area of formwork? See sketch below.

No, voids ≤ 5m² are not deducted, Measurement Rule E20.M8.

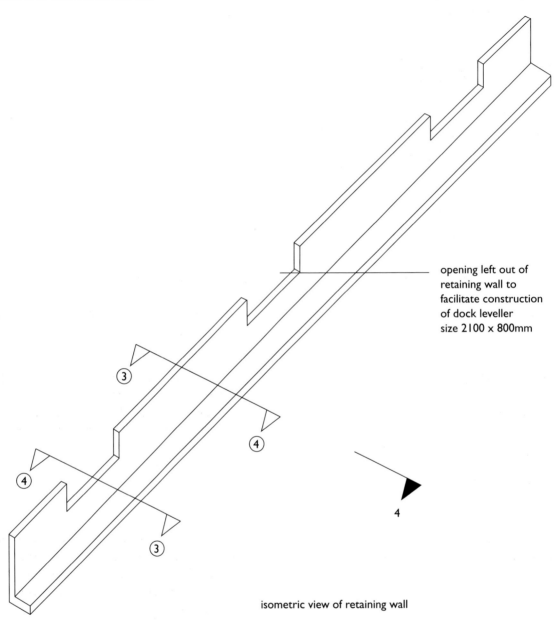

opening left out of retaining wall to facilitate construction of dock leveller size 2100 x 800mm

isometric view of retaining wall

▶ A suspended slab is formed with 50mm thick precast concrete decking and 150mm thick in situ concrete to form a 200mm overall thick composite deck construction. Projecting below the decking is a reinforced concrete beam. What formwork should be measured to the beam sides and soffit as indicated by the dotted line?

Formwork for the beam described would be measured to exposed sides and soffit requiring temporary support, E20.M1. The downstand beam is formed by temporary formwork and the slab is supported by permanent formwork, therefore the downstand beam is regarded as an isolated beam, E20.D9.

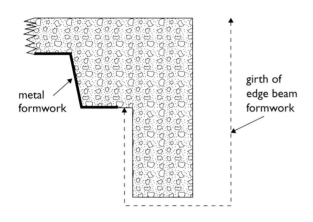

metal formwork

girth of edge beam formwork

▶ The finished surface of a concrete slab soffit is described as 'finished fair'. How should the formwork be measured?

Fair finish to surface of concrete is measured either as extra over basic finish formwork, E20.1–5 or formwork may be described as 'fair finish formwork'.

▶ When measuring a reinforced concrete wall the specification refers to kickerless construction for formwork, consequently there is not an item in the BoQ for wall kickers. Should there still be an item measured in the BoQ under SMM7 for wall kickers or would they be deemed to be included in the item for formwork to walls?

SMM7 rules require work to be measured in accordance with the drawings and specification. If the design specifies kickerless construction, formwork to kickers cannot be measured.

▶ Does a 'fix only' Bill item for holding down bolts include forming the mortice?

No, an item for forming mortices to receive holding down bolts should be measured as E20.26.1.1. The qualification or definition of 'fix only' cannot include forming of a mortice in another trade.

▶ Should the use of formwork to the edges of slabs be left to the discretion of the contractor where the slab abuts new buildings, kerbs and walls, and therefore treated as a 'risk' item?

Formwork is not a risk item. It is measured to concrete surfaces requiring temporary support during casting, E20.M1. It is not measured if not used.

▶ Please explain the measurement of passings.

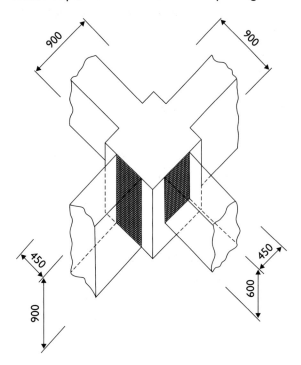

Measurement Rule E20.M3 states that 'passings of ground beams are not deducted from area of formwork'. This means that no deduction is made from the area of formwork to the side of a ground beam where the end of an abutting ground beam meets the side of another ground beam or the side of a pile cap, as illustrated by the shaded areas.

▶ Please define slabs and beams as referred to in SMM7.

Definitions of slabs and beams contained in Definition Rules E10.D4(a) and D7 follow through to the measurement rules of formwork. The structural engineer's opinion or description of a structural member cannot overrule the SMM definitions of beams, slabs, etc.

▶ Plywood was used to support concrete temporarily. Should this be measured as formwork?

Yes, if plywood was needed to support concrete then it must be measured as formwork. If permanent, it must be described as permanent formwork.

▶ A typical column shape is cast prior to a connecting beam being formed through the step formed at column head.

Is this detail measurable as a complex shape?

The step detail at the top of the circular column would be described as a rebate and the forming of such should be measured as 'extra over the formwork in which it occurs' in accordance with E20.19.1.

▶ This query relates to the construction of a one-sided shutter to the internal face of an upstand. The Bill item reads 'fair faced formwork upstand n.e. 150mm high'.

● Please confirm if the item should have been described as one-sided and so measured?

● When does an upstand become a wall?

● E20 has no specific requirement for formwork to sides of upstands to be either one- or two-sided, each specific item should be described as designed or executed.

● When an upstand becomes a wall depends on its intended function in the finished structure. This should be left to the discretion of the surveyor.

▶ Are cambers in formwork measured?

If the finished soffit of the concrete slab is to be level, the formwork would not be described as cambered.

If the finished soffit is to retain the camber, then yes.

▶ Can you explain the various height requirements of formwork, especially in relation to the differing heights to soffits.

The formwork heights are described as illustrated:

a)   slabs ≤ 1.50m and then thereafter in 1.50m stages (H1);

b)   walls that exceed 3m in height require a separate item from walls that do not exceed 3m;

c)   beams ≤ 1.50m and then thereafter in 1.50m stages (H2);

d)   columns that exceed 3m in height require a separate item from columns that do not exceed 3m.

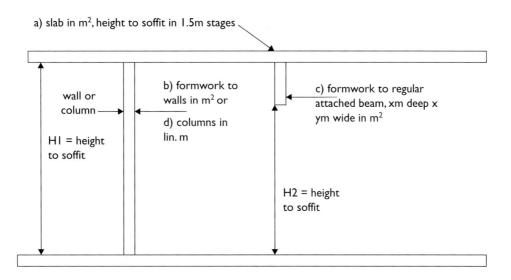

a) slab in m², height to soffit in 1.5m stages

wall or column →

H1 = height to soffit

b) formwork to walls in m² or

d) columns in lin. m

c) formwork to regular attached beam, xm deep x ym wide in m²

H2 = height to soffit

▶ How should formwork be measured to the soffit of a 250mm thick slab with a thickened deep portion, 650mm thick in the middle?

Soffit to slabs 200–300mm thick in m² as E20.8.2.

Soffit to slabs 600–700mm thick in m² as E20.8.2.

Plus an item for:

Steps in soffit; plain; vertical; height 250–500. (in linear metres).

▶ Should column kickers be treated like wall kickers?

No, a column kicker is not a measurable item. E20 does not include a rule for the measurement of column kickers because the formwork items for the columns must state the number of columns measured, E20.15 and 16, therefore the contractor can allow in the formwork rate for column kickers.

# SMM7 Q & A

▶ What defines the difference between an upstand and a wall or alternatively when does an upstand become a wall?

E20 does not contain any specific definition of upstands or walls. They are defined by the purpose for which they were designed.

▶ Is the area of formwork to a concrete wall deemed to be 'to both sides', i.e. 1m$^2$ of formwork in the BoQ equates to 2m$^2$ of wall formwork?

No, formwork must be measured to each face that requires temporary support during construction, Measurement Rule E20.M1.

▶ How should formwork to a concrete wall with an attached column projecting from one side be measured?

It should be measured as follows:
- formwork to walls to the side without the attached column, as E20.12.*.1–2;
- interrupted formwork to walls to the side with the attached column, as E20.12.*.1–2.2;
- formwork to attached columns, as E20.15.1.

▶ The specification for formwork to a concrete suspended slab states that the formwork should be laid with an upward camber to ensure that the top finished soffit should be horizontal after the formwork is struck.

Should the formwork be measured as 'cambered' rather than 'horizontal'?

No.

▶ Please clarify where under SMM7 we are entitled to be paid for cutting formwork panels to accommodate the protrusion of the water pipes.

The rules of Work Section E20 do not contain an item for cutting formwork to accommodate protruding pipes. Coverage Rule C1 applies. For this Coverage Rule to apply however, the contractor must be made aware of the presence of these pipes at tender stage, thereby allowing the contractor to include the cost of adapting the formwork within the general rates for formwork.

▶ Are kickers to upstands measured?

No.

▶ What is a 'deep beam'?

A deep beam is one whose depth (measured below the slab where attached) is greater than three times its width, Definition Rule E10.D7. Formwork to a deep beam is also measured from below the slab.

▶ How is the fixing of 'holding down bolts' measured?

This work is enumerated and measured in accordance with E42.1.*.1.

Measure a mortice as E20.26 if the bolts are to be set into preformed mortices.

▶ Should formwork be measured to sides of grout under stanchion bases?

Not unless it has been specifically specified. Usually it is left to the discretion of the contractor how the column base is grouted.

▶ When is 'Basic finish formwork' not at the contractor's discretion?

How do you ascertain the principal type of formwork?

Basic formwork is not at the conractor's discretion when the drawings and/or specification state otherwise. Generally the principal type of formwork would be that with the greatest area.

▶ What is the definition of interrupted formwork as referred to in rule E20.12.–.1–2.2?

Interrupted formwork is an area of wall formwork interrupted by projections such as full height openings, attached columns, piers, beams, floor slabs or the like. The sketches that were included in the Practice Manual that accompanied SMM6 as reproduced below best illustrate the term.

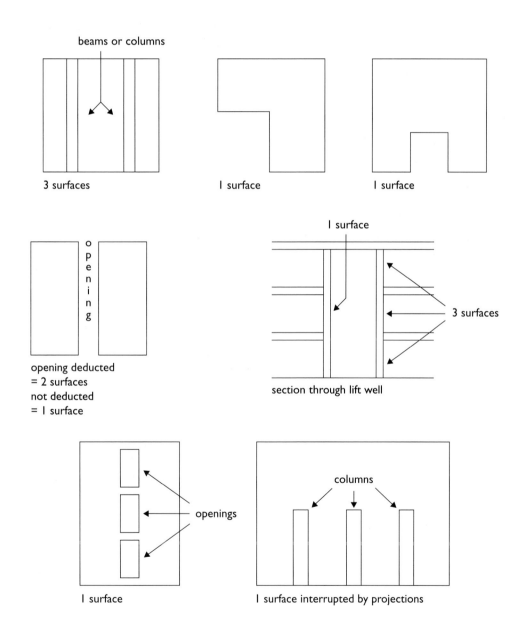

beams or columns

3 surfaces

1 surface

1 surface

opening

opening deducted
= 2 surfaces
not deducted
= 1 surface

1 surface

3 surfaces

section through lift well

openings

1 surface

columns

1 surface interrupted by projections

▶ Should separate items for formwork to cased beams be measured from the formwork for concrete walls if steel beams are contained within the walls and all formwork is in the same plane?

No, if the formwork remains in the same plane, there is no requirement to measure separate formwork items. Drawn information must be provided with the BoQ, showing the relative positions of differing types of construction as required by E20.P1(a) and G10.P1.

# E30 Reinforcement for in situ concrete

▶ What is the definition of 'at the discretion of the contractor', i.e. should chairs be measured to support top layer of steel?

This phrase means that the method of carrying out the work described in the Bill item is left entirely to the contractor, who can use whatever method he or she wishes subject to normal restrictions relating to building regulations and 'good practice'.

▶ How are chairs and spacers measured?

The weight of spacers and chairs which are not at the discretion of the contractor must be included in the quantities of reinforcement.

Chairs must be measured if their material, shape, size or position is not left to the discretion of the contractor.

# E40 Designed joints in in situ concrete

▶ ● Under which SMM rule can cutting of the edge of existing concrete be measured?

● Items for breaking out existing concrete slabs are measured in accordance with D20.4 and 5, describing the method of cutting.

● Does the word 'cut' under E40 describe a 'saw cutting' of the edge of existing concrete slab?

● No, in this context the word cut refers to how a construction joint is to be formed in a new slab.

● Is it correct to describe insertion of vertical dowel bars at the underside of a new reinforced concrete beam as a 'horizontal joint with dowel bars'?

● No, dowel bars inserted into new concrete would be enumerated with a dimensioned description in accordance with E42.1.

▶ The joints in a concrete slab or pool base are designed by the structural engineer and shown on the drawings. A note on the drawing states that the positions shown for the joints are provisional and that the exact positions can be left to the discretion of the contractor to suit the preferred concrete pouring programme. Are some or all of these joints measurable?

The joints should be measured in accordance with E40.1–3.1–2.1 but described as 'provisional'. The completed work should then be remeasured as executed.

▶ What is the exact meaning of Measurement Rule E40.M3 with specific reference to the word 'only'? Surely all angles or intersections should be measured.

No, the word 'only' means that there is no need to measure an angle in a preformed waterstop if the construction is so simple that the angle in the waterstop can be formed simply by bending it.

▶ Is a joint between the edge of a concrete slab and a concrete wall measurable?

It is only measurable if it is a designed joint.

▶ A specification states that a concrete slab must be poured in bays not exceeding 30m². The method of forming the joint separating the bays is left to the discretion of the contractor. Should these joints be measured?

No, it is left to the contractor to lay the concrete in whichever sequence suits the construction programme therefore the exact spacing of day-to-day construction joints is left to the contractor's discretion.

A concrete specification describes the exact method of forming a day-to-day construction joint but the spacing is left to the discretion of the contractor. Is this joint measurable?

Yes, a provisional quantity would be measured in the BoQ and subsequently remeasured on completion.

# E41  Worked finishes/Cutting to in situ concrete

▶ Abrasive blasting/pneumatic scabbling has not been measured under Work Section E41. The specification for Work Sections M10 and M20 refer to abrasive blasting/pneumatic scabbling. Is this treatment therefore deemed included in the Bill items or are these composite items contrary to General Rule 4.2?

General Rule 4.2 means that treatment to surface of concrete slabs must be measured separately in accordance with E41.6 or 7. This work can only be included in Work Section M10 or M20 if the Bill items have been clearly 'qualified' somewhere in the tender document.

▶ Should an item be measured under Work Section E41 for finishing the top surface of a slab to camber?

Yes, E41.1–7.*.*. to cambers.

# E42  Accessories cast into in situ concrete

▶ Please confirm whether the following are measurable items and if so, where they are measured within SMM7?
● bolt jigs; and
● filling mortices formed during the installation of bolt jigs.

Bolt jigs would be deemed included within item E42.1. It is left to the discretion of the contractor how bolts are held in position whilst being cast in.

Filling mortices in foundation bases is measured under E10.17.1.

# E60 Precast/Composite concrete decking

▶ *Precast concrete floor units*

These are the normal precast concrete wide slab floors (approx. 1200mm wide) available from several manufacturers. The BoQ measures these in accordance with SMM Section E50.

All steelwork drawings showing beams, columns and span of floors were sent out as part of the tender documents.

The contractor states that he is entitled to payment for notching the ends (usually corners) of the units for steel columns. There is no indication in the SMM that this is a measurable item. It is our view that it is not measurable and was apparent from the tender drawings.

Precast concrete floor units – notching ends of a precast concrete floor unit is a measurable item, E50.2.4.

▶ *Precast concrete wall units*

Can a wall comprising two precast concrete skins infilled with reinforced in situ concrete be measured in the BoQ as a composite item in m$^2$ therefore using rules similar to composite floors as Work Section E60?

Yes, in the absence of specific rules for composite walls, General Rule 11.1 permits the surveyor to use similar provided this fact is clearly stated in the BoQ.

▶ Should precast prestressed hollow floor slabs be measured under Work Section E50 or E60?

They should be measured under Work Section E60, as described in the *Common Arrangement of Work Sections* (CAWS).

# F Masonry

## F10 Brick/Block walling

## F11 Glass block walling

▶ Should fair cutting and fair angles be measured when measuring quantities of fair faced blockwork?

No, fair cutting, etc. is deemed included unless the blockwork has been designed and specified to be used without cutting.

▶ Must ornamental facework bands be measured full value or extra over the work in which they occur?

They can be measured either as full value as F10.13.1–3.1–4 or as extra over in accordance with F10.13.1–3.1–4.1.

▶ A skin of 100mm thick concrete blockwork with 45mm thick insulation bonded to it has to be measured. What thickness of wall should be given in the Bill description?

It should be 100mm – this is the thickness of the structural element of the item. Reference to the bonded insulation must also be given in the Bill description as required by Supplementary Information item F10.S1.

▶ In situ concrete, 300mm thick, was placed between two skins of 100mm thick blockwork. Should the blockwork be described as 'used for formwork'?

Yes, in accordance with F10.1.1.1.3.

▶ There is an anomaly between Definition Rule F10.D3 and the word 'vertical' in the third column of Classification Rule F10.1–3.1.1.

The word 'vertical' appears in column three to ensure that all descriptions comply with the requirement of General Rule 2.6, namely every description shall identify the work with respect to one descriptive feature drawn from each of the first three columns in the Classification Table. This was especially important when setting up computerised billing programmes.

▶ Facing brickwork was specified to be built in 'English' bond. This will require the use of 'Queen closer' bricks. Should these bricks be measured extra over the work in which they occur as 'special' bricks in accordance with F10.11.1?

No, Queen closer bricks must always adjoin the quoin header in English bond and would therefore be considered standard when building facing brickwork in English bond. They should not be measured as 'specials'.

Please define what cutting of facing brickwork is measurable when measuring faced arches.

All rough and fair cutting is deemed included as stated in Coverage Rule F10.C1(b).

▶ Should facing brick copings which contain horizontal, vertical and curved bands be measured along the centre of their face line, separated into vertical, curved, etc. or is it in order to measure one horizontal item with reference to a drawing, i.e. the X dimension in the diagram?

They should be measured as the mean girth on face with separate items for horizontal, vertical or curved work as F10.17.1.1–4.

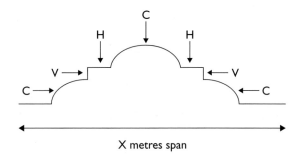

X metres span

▶ How should a skin of brickwork built around a steel column but tied to the main wall be measured? See sketch below.

The rules of F30 should be adapted slightly. This brickwork should be described as 'walls, attached casings'.

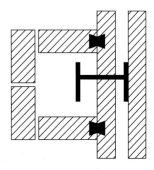

▶ We would welcome your opinion on how to measure a detail as shown on the sketch. We are unsure whether to measure it as:

(a) a 325mm wall with a separate item for 'extra over forming 100mm recess' giving the recess area or size; or

(b) a 325mm wall and a 225mm wall separately without reference to the recess; or

(c) a 325mm wall, a 225mm wall and a further item for forming the recess.

Both thicknesses are the same height.

The brickwork described in your letter should be measured as described in option (b) but with the additional information added to the description to fully describe the situation, complexity, etc.

This may be done by reference to a drawing or detail.

The rules of all work sections state that certain drawings must accompany the BoQs. General Rule 1.1 states 'more detailed information than is required by these rules shall be given where necessary in order to define the precise nature and extent of the required work'.

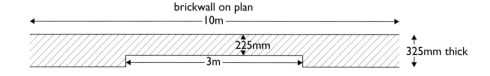

brickwall on plan
10m
225mm
3m
325mm thick

▶ A wall is constructed in 440mm thick brickwork for the first 1m of height and reduces to 215mm thick for the remaining 2m of height. The 215mm thick wall contains 440mm long attached piers projecting 225mm from one side of the wall at 2.4m centres. Should the brickwork at these piers be measured as 440mm thick walls?

No, the masonry should be measured as follows:
- The 1m high lower part of the wall as 'walls, 440mm thick', in m²; F10.1.1.1.
- The 2m upper part of the wall as 'walls, 215mm thick', in m²; F10.1.1.1.
- The attached piers as 'projections, 440mm long x 225mm projection, vertical', in linear metres; F10.5.1.1, the length of each pier being 2m.

▶ A wall is constructed in facing bricks as the sketch below. It is generally 215mm thick faced both sides but contains piers to both faces of the wall that are constructed in a different coloured facing brick. The piers differ in length, some being longer than 4 times their thickness. The total thickness of brickwork at the position of the piers is 440mm. Should these piers be measured as walls, isolated piers or projections?

The piers that are ≤ four times their thickness are measured as projections in linear metres giving their width, depth of projection and description of the facing brick from which they are constructed as F10.5.1.1.

The piers that are longer than four times their thickness are measured as 440mm thick walls faced both sides giving the type of facing brick in the description as F10.1.1.1.

It is essential that drawn information accompanies the Bills of quantities in order to illustrate this situation, as required by Rule F10.P1 (a) and (b).

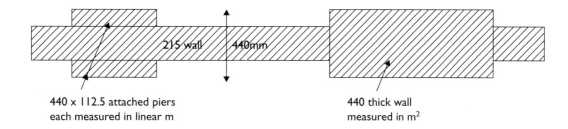

440 x 112.5 attached piers
each measured in linear m

440 thick wall
measured in m²

▶ *Radius works*

Brick walls are built to varying radii, ranging from 2–3m.

Should the brick-on-edge and coping, tile creasing and cavity trays also be measured and described as 'built to radius'?

Any work built to a radius must be so described, F10.M4, with the radius stated.

▶ *Cavity*

The wall is tied to the concrete core and we are required to maintain a 20mm cavity between the wall and this core. We believe this should be measured under F30.1.2, please confirm.

The 20mm cavity should be measured in accordance with F30.1.2.1.

# SMM7 Q & A

▶ Please define 'rough' and 'fair' cutting to blockwork and 'special' brick?

Rough and fair cutting is any cutting of new bricks and blocks either within the thickness of the work or at boundaries and edges of new work that is necessary.

A special brick is a brick that is not a standard regular size whole, half or quarter.

▶ Why do the rules of SMM7 not allow the measurement of rough or fair cutting of brickwork or blockwork?

Square, rough and fair cutting is deemed included in brickwork and blockwork because the rules require certain drawn information to accompany the BoQs, F10.P1.

If the thickness and heights of brickwork and blockwork have not changed since tender, then all square, rough and fair cutting will be deemed included within the tender rates. It does not matter whether the information is shown on the architect's or engineer's drawings as long as the information shown is consistent.

Should a separate item be measured for infill to steel columns?

There is no requirement within SMM7 to measure a separate item for blockwork which has been reduced in thickness to fit into web of steel column.

Should curved cutting work to form curved reveals, which will be covered by render, be deemed included as rough and fair cutting under F10.C1 or measured linear under F10.10?

All rough and fair cutting to brickwork or blockwork is deemed included, F10.C1(b).

Are quoin blocks measured as an extra over to facing blockwork?

Quoin blocks should be measured separately in linear metres if the blocks differ from general facing blocks.

Is a block on end course measured as an extra over to facing blockwork?

A block on end course should be measured as an extra over item as a flush band F10.13.

Are reveal blocks at openings an extra over to facing blockwork?

Purpose made reveal blocks should be measured as special blocks as F10.11.1.1.

Should fair cutting be measured where ends and tops of a facing brick skin abut a concrete column or beam?

No.

Does a change in the specification after tender of a facing blockwork, or its place of manufacture, constitute a change to the BoQ item?

Yes.

Should 'rough cutting' to blockwork be measured?

No, see Coverage Rule F10.C1(b).

# F20 Natural stone rubble walling

▶ Walls have been specified to be built in stone salvaged from demolitions. This means that they must be cut to suit the specified bed thickness of the new stonewalls. Should this cutting be measured separately?

No, all rough and fair cutting of stone to give a correct bed thickness is deemed included within the item for a stone wall, Coverage Rule F20.C1(i), because the average bed thickness must be given in the Bill description.

Other stones salvaged from the demolitions have to be cut to size to form jamb stones. Should this cutting be measured separately?

No, the Bill item must give a dimensioned description, F20.11.1–3.1.

▶ How is a tooled margin (as shown in sketch) to a quoin or a jamb measured?

F20.C1(h) states that 'dressed margins to rubble work' are deemed included.

Quoin stones should be measured full value in linear metres as F20.10.1.1.

Tooled margins are deemed included.

Jamb stones should be measured full value in linear metres as F20.11.1.1.

Tooled margins are deemed included.

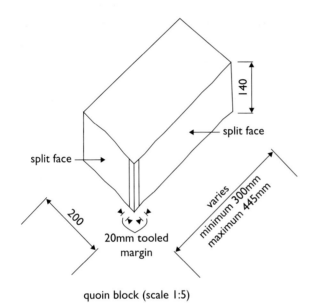

split face

split face

140

200

20mm tooled margin

varies minimum 300mm maximum 445mm

quoin block (scale 1:5)

# F21 Natural stone ashlar walling/dressings

▶ How are 90° angles in horizontal band courses of natural stone to be measured?

Blocks forming 90° mitred angles in band courses should be itemised as 'special purpose stones' and described as 'angle blocks', in accordance with F21.33.1.1–2.

▶ How are stones of a length at variance with a standard size so set out for aesthetic reasons to be measured?

Stones of a length at variance with standard size block would be measured in accordance with F21.33.1.2 and described as 'bonder blocks'.

▶ Is it essential to describe mouldings as Measurement Rule M7 or will the typical section sketches on tender drawings suffice? Does the billed item need to contain the drawing reference or section reference in the description or heading?

The Bill description can either fully describe all mouldings or refer to a drawing or sketch.

▶ Do special cut bonder blocks within an ashlar wall of uniform thickness necessitated by aesthetic requirements with regard to perpendicular joint locations fall into the classification 1.1.1 (walls of stated thickness, vertical) or are they to be classed as 'special purpose block'?

Special cut bonder blocks must be itemised separately as 'special purpose blocks', in accordance with F21.33.1.1–2.

## F22 Cast stone ashlar walling/dressings

▶ BoQ descriptions and specifications state reconstituted stonework is designed to be used without cutting and that all fair cutting is to be deemed included. Subsequently fair cutting becomes necessary due to coordination problems.

Yes.

Should this fair cutting be measured?

## F30 Accessories/Sundry items for brick/block/stone walling

▶ Should a separate item be measured for dressing a damp course at floor level and cavity trays at high level around steel columns?

The rules of Work Section F30 of SMM7 do not require an item be measured for dressing damp-proof courses around steel columns provided the drawings clearly show the relationship between the steelwork and the dpcs.

▶ Should designed joints in brickwork be measured for the following situations (see sketches)?

Yes, in accordance with F30.8.1, provided they are not at the discretion of the contractor.

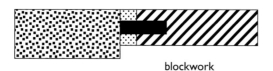

concrete          blockwork

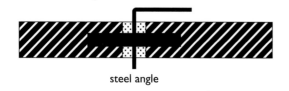

steel angle

▶ Should ends, angles and intersections in in-situ, preformed or prefabricated cavity trays be measured?

The rules of Work Section F30 do not contain items for ends, angles and intersections in in-situ, preformed or prefabricated cavity trays therefore they are not measurable.

In accordance with General Rule 1.1 it would not be incorrect to measure them because of, say, their complexity or excessive number.

# G Structural/Carcassing metal/timber

## G10 Structural steel framing

## G11 Structural aluminium framing

## G12 Isolated structural metal members

▶ Steel plates are welded to structural steel members. These plates are to provide a fixing for the ends of timber rafters. Should these plates be measured as 'fittings' in Work Section G10 or as 'metal connectors' in Work Section G20?

They should be measured as 'fittings' in accordance with G10.1.10 and Measurement Rules G10.M1 and M2.

▶ Should steel members and fittings used to connect new steelwork to existing steelwork be measured separately from the new steelwork?

No, the preamble to the measured items must make reference to the drawings used to measure the steelwork with special reference to the areas where new steel is to be connected to existing steel as required by G10.P1.

▶ Should the inside surface of a hollow steel section be included in the superficial area measured for galvanising?

If yes, what rules of measurement apply?

Yes, if the specification requires the inside surface to be coated.

In the absence of specific rules in Work Section G10, General Rule 11.1 states that such rules, as far as possible, shall conform to similar rules given for similar work. In this case the rules from Work Section M60 would apply with particular reference given in the Bill description to the fact that the coating must be applied to the inside of a hollow section.

▶ Should the weight of 'cold rolled purlins and cladding rails' be added to the overall mass of structural steel that is included in the item of 'permanent erection on site', G10.2.2?

No, cold rolled purlins and cladding rails are measured in linear metres in accordance with G10.4.1.

Erection is deemed included in this item.

▶ When calculating the mass of steel section with flanges and webs of different thicknesses, which thickness is used to calculate the mass of the steel section as per Measurement Rule G10.M5, i.e. 785kg/m$^2$ per 100mm thickness?

The exact area of the section is calculated and then multiplied by its length in order to calculate the volume of the member in m$^3$. The volume of the member is then multiplied by 7.85 tonnes/m$^3$.

▶ Should 'sitework' on existing steelwork be deemed included in the measured items of a new isolated steel member being attached to existing structural steel?

No, sitework (i.e. drilling holes) to existing steelwork should be measured separately.

▶ Should the weight of haunches on portal frames be included in the overall mass of steel measured in a BoQ or are they classified as fittings?

They are a component part of the portal frame and their mass would be included in the overall weight of structural steel.

▶ Where the members of a steel built-up girder truss change size and proportions after tender, should the trusses be remeasured and their weight recalculated to enable the rate to be adjusted?

Yes, it would be reasonable to recalculate their weight and consequently adjust their rate.

▶ Structural steel members have been described as 'plain isolated structural members'. When incorporated into the building they are actually bolted together. Should they have been described as fabricated steel with separate items measured for 'fabrication' and 'erection'?

Yes.

▶ We have had some difficulty in assessing the allowance made within this section of the Bill for carrying our work to the existing building.

This work includes site drilling/welding of existing cold rolled steel members and making connections for new steelwork.

We are of the opinion that any works to existing structures should be individually categorised as a separate item in the Bill, however, under this section there is no reference to any such works.

All work that occurs on, in or immediately under work existing before the current project must be described as 'Work to existing buildings' – see General Rules 13.1, 13.2 and 13.3.

**Haunches to columns**

The steel columns for the project are designed with a curved eaves detail which, because of the radii involved, are required to be fabricated out of steel plate. The items in question are measured in tonnes and described in the Contract Bills as:

'Haunches; fabricated from steel into universal beam section tapering in depth from 790 to 610; overall length approximately 3000; consisting of 20 thick web plate, 32 thick x 229 wide flange plates; curved in profile; as drawing no. [XX].'

- Should the curved web be measured as the net area of steel designed and weighted up accordingly and, if so, should the description clarify that it is the net weight that has been calculated; or

- should the curved web be measured as the smallest rectangular plate from which the web can be cut, having regard for Measurement Rule M3 of section G which would seem to indicate there should be no deductions for splay cuts, etc.; or

- is there any other guidance as to how the tonnage billed should be calculated?

General Rule 3.1 states 'work shall be measured net as fixed in position'. The weight is to be calculated from the designed size of the haunch. It would not be incorrect to state this in the Bill item.

## Galvanising to cold rolled sections

The purlins and cladding rails are specified as a proprietary zed sleeved system and the preambles make it clear that proprietary products are to be installed strictly in accordance with the manufacturer's recommendations.

The manufacturer's product literature identifies that the zed sleeved system members are hot dipped galvanised.

The items are billed in linear metres and described as:

'Cold rolled sections: Zed sleeved system; bolted site connections; in accordance with the manufacturer's instructions. Purlins and cladding rails ref: 262 Z 23.'

- Should an item for galvanising be measured as per G10.8.1; or

- should the item description state the members are to be galvanised?

Galvanising should be measured as G10.8.1 unless the reference number refers only to a galvanised member. If this is the case the description would comply with General Rule 6.1 and the member would be deemed to be galvanised.

## Brackets for cold rolled sections

The zed sections referred to above are attached to the structural frame via a series of proprietary brackets and the same brackets are also used to provide continuity of the rails in the running length.

Is the description given above adequate to include these brackets, or should they be measured separately as fittings under G10.1.10?

Weight of brackets should be included in measurement of fittings, G10.1.10, or if proprietary they could be enumerated and the manufacturer's reference number stated in accordance with G.10.1.12.

# SMM7 Q & A

## Curved/pre-cambered trusses

The roof to the building incorporates a series of built-up trusses.

The fabrication is billed in tonnes and described as:

'Trusses and built-up girders generally; weight over 40kg/m but not exceeding 100kg/m.'

The drawing indicates that the top section of the truss is curved and the note indicates that it is to have a pre-camber. The drawing also indicates that whilst the bottom boom is straight in its completed condition, the member is to be fabricated with a specified pre-camber.

Having regard to items G10.1.8.1 and 4, should the description state that the top boom is curved and should the description also state that the truss is pre-cambered, or alternatively are the works adequately described?

The Bill description should include the word 'cambered' as G10.1.8.2.3 and 4.

## Holding down bolt assemblies

The holding down bolt assemblies are enumerated and described as:

'Holding down bolt assemblies; drawing no. [XX] including plates, bolts, washers, nuts, etc. Base plate type BPI; reference BSI.'

- Is the description as billed adequate to include the base plate within the item; or
- should the base plate be weighted up and included within the fabrication, erection and surface treatment items for the columns to which it is welded?

The description is adequate to include the base plate.

## Fittings – What constitutes a fitting?

- Is a haunch a fitting or to be weighted as part of the rafter as a main member?

- Are such items as shelf angles fittings or main members as they do not connect the structural steel together but are for other trades to connect their work to?

- Net areas. A haunch is made up of steel plate, should it be measured as the net area or the gross area, i.e. the smallest piece of steel we can cut the plate from?

- A haunch is not a fitting, but a component. Its mass is included with the associated beam or column, G10.M1.

- Shelf angles are fittings, as are brackets, cleats, supports, etc. used to support services.

- The mass of an irregular shaped member is the net weight and is calculated from net area of the haunch. Reference to splay cuts in G10.M3 is only for assessing length of steel members that have splayed ends. It does not relate to irregular shaped members.

The contractor says that under G10.P1 the QS must either:

- refer to location drawings in the prelims; or
- refer to drawings accompanying the BoQ.

Must this information be provided with the tender document?

Yes, otherwise the measurement of structural steel does not fully comply with SMM7 G10.

▶ Please clarify provisional quantities.

Any Bill item described as 'provisional' must be treated as such and the quantity will be subject to remeasurement on completion of the work. If a quantity cannot be accurately determined, an estimate of quantity shall be given and identified as an approximate quantity. The term of 'provisional' is one method of describing a quantity as approximate.

▶ Should the weight of fittings be measured separately from that of the main structural steelwork?

Yes, in accordance with G10.1.10.

▶ Should the mass of fittings be added to that of the main structural steelwork for the 'erection' item?

Yes, the weight of all items listed from G10.1 to G10.10 should be added together for the 'erection' item G10.2.

▶ Do you have to stipulate in BoQ descriptions that a beam or column is of the cellular type?

If a type of member not listed in G10.1 needs to be measured then it must be so described. The lists are not exhaustive.

▶ Please define the measurement of fittings.

Fittings are all those items needed to connect the various steel members. Their weights are all added together as required by Measurement Rule M2. This would apply to contractor-designed fittings.

Isolated steel members and their fittings are measured separately in accordance with G10.5.1–3.

▶ Should 'connections' between steel members be measured?

No, all fittings used in making connections are grouped together and measured in tonnes. This applies equally to connections between new steel and between new and existing steel members.

When are steel members considered 'fabricated' or 'plain isolated'?

Drawing shows a variety of steel beams and columns. Some are clearly 'plain isolated' but others are loose at one end and bolted to a steel column at the other end.

If two or more beams, columns, etc. are connected to each other they are no longer isolated, therefore they should be described as fabricated and measured in accordance with G10.1.

▶ Please define the measurement of loose steel purlins.

Steel roof purlins laid across walls and not 'framed' are 'isolated structural members'. Bolted connections in the running length of a member does not mean that the steelwork should be considered as framed structural steelwork.

▶ What is meant by a 'built-up member' as referred to in G10.1.7 and 8 and G10.5.2?

Built-up columns and girders refer to structurally integrated members fabricated from more than one structural member to form a single column or beam.

▶ Please provide clarification on the most appropriate method of measurement under SMM7 in each of the following instances:

- Galvanised steel frames which are fixed to a concrete backing (measured elsewhere) and provide support to the windows (provided by others). The steel frames consist mainly of rolled steel angle, with additional angles welded on, all with a weight ≤ 40kg/m. The frames are rectangular and repeat throughout the building, having been prefabricated off site.

- Galvanised steel framing to window openings can be measured under G12.1 I suggest that galvanised steel frames be described as 'composite' items and therefore 'numbered'.

- In order to prevent water ingress between two parallel steel angles, which are welded or bolted together, the architect has shown a continuous fillet weld or a seal weld, which is not required for structural purposes. How would you recommend that the welds are measured?

- I suggest that a 'rogue' item be composed to measure and describe non-structural welds and that this work be measured either in linear metres for continuous welds or enumerated for short lengths.

# G20 Carpentry/Timber framing/First fixing

▶ Are timber head and sole plates in proprietary partitions deemed included as components of the partition or should they be measured separately?

They should be measured separately as butt jointed supports, G20.11.

▶ Softwood plates are fixed to structural steel beams by bolting. The holes in the steel are to be drilled on site.

Should the drilling on site be measured under G10 or G20?

The drilling of the steel is deemed included in the measured items for bolts, G20.2.1, Coverage Rule C3, provided all relevant information has been given as required by the SMM7 rules.

▶ Should separate items be measured for timber grounds that are plugged and screwed to brickwork, cinder blockwork or concrete?

Not unless different types of fixings are required or the methods of fixing are not left to the discretion of the contractor, G20.S2.

► The drawing shows a timber purlin to be made up of two identically sized sections of laminated timber. Should this purlin be measured as one composite member or twice times the basic piece of laminated timber that makes up the purlin?

The purlin should be measured and described as a composite member giving the overall finished size but stating the size and number of pieces used to make up the purlin.

The drawing of a metal stud partition shows several IPS panels. The detail shows the IPS panels clipped to a 100mm x 50mm softwood subframe that is fixed to the metal studs. Would this subframe be deemed included in the Bill item for the IPS panels?

No, they should be measured as 'individual supports' in accordance with G20.13 and Definition Rule G20.D7.

► Timber members are described as being 'bolted to steel with M10 bolts'. Does this description mean that the bolts and the drilling of holes through the timber and steel are all deemed included?

The bolts must be measured separately in accordance with G20.25.1.

Drilling holes through the timber is deemed included in the item for the timber member as Coverage Rule G20.C1.

Drilling holes through the steel is deemed included in the item for the bolts as Coverage Rule G20.C3.

► Timber members are described as being 'bolted to steel with M10 bolts'. Should separate items be measured for drilling holes through structural steel members that are drilled off site and on site?

No, drilling holes through the steel is deemed included in the item for the bolts as Coverage Rule G20.C3. It is left to the discretion of the contractor whether the holes are drilled on or off site.

► A Bill description of a glued laminated timber beam makes no reference to several notches and splayed ends. No dimensioned diagram is given.

Should these labours be described in the BoQ item?

The labours would be deemed included as stated in Coverage Rule G20.C1. To allow the cost of these labours to be included in the truss items they must either be described in the Bill item or shown on a drawing or dimensioned diagram that must accompany the BoQ.

► A BoQ contains measured items for glued laminated timber beams and rafters and refers to specific drawings.

Would the valley rafters be deemed included within the items and rates of principal members if shown on the drawings but not specifically measured in the BoQ?

No, valley rafters must be measured as G20.9.2 and Definition Rule G20.D6.

► Should an item of 'hoisting and setting in position' be measured for roof trusses that, because of their design, the QS measured their individual timbers in linear metres, assuming they would be fabricated on site at ground level and subsequently hoisted and set in position?

In accordance with General Rule 1.1, yes, in order to provide more detailed information than is required by the rules.

This method of measuring the trusses should be stated in a qualification to the rules.

# SMM7 Q & A

▶ Is a subcontractor entitled to payment for notching ends of joists into webs of steels?

All work in G20 is deemed to include labours on items of timber. The rules do not require notching ends of timber to be measured, therefore the cost of these labours is deemed included within rate for joists.

▶ Is a subcontractor entitled to payment for treating cut ends of joists?

Treating cut ends of joists is deemed included.

▶ Should all carcassing works to octagonal roofs be measured as 'irregular' shaped areas?

Drawings must accompany the Bills of quantities to define the scope and location of the work, Information Rule G10.P1. This will alert the contractor to an irregular shaped roof.

Principal members of all roofs, no matter what shape, are measured in accordance with G20.9.1 or 2.1 and as defined in Definition Rules D5 and D6.

Supports, gutterboards, cleats, etc. are measured in accordance with G20.11–18 and, if forming part of an irregular shaped area, it will be stated in the description.

▶ The notching of joists is measured within the Bill items of roof timbers but not for the floor joists, etc.

Should notches in the floor joists be measured?

G20.C1 states 'The work is deemed to include labours on items of timber, except as otherwise required'. The rules of Work Section G20 do not require notches to be measured. Forming a notch is a labour not a method of fixing, therefore forming a notch is deemed included.

▶ How are softwood noggings fixed between timber joists to support edges of plasterboard sheet measured?

They can be measured as individual supports in accordance with G20.13.*.1.

▶ Items have been measured under G20 Carpentry/Timber framing/First fixing and have been described as 'beams', 'heads', 'posts', etc. The only labours measured are splays, chamfers, etc. within the item description apart from several enumerated items for 'housed ends'.

The timber framing described would be measured in linear metres or square metres as framed supports, in accordance with G20.12.1–2.1.1–5. All labours would be deemed included.

Please advise if the required mortice and tenon joints and dowelled joints should be measured separately as numbered items?

The type of fixings and jointing mentioned would be given in the description as required by Supplementary Information item G20.S9.

▶ If timber grounds are shown in a manufacturer's installation guide or the drawn details of a proprietary partition system, are they deemed included as a component of a proprietary partition system as required by Coverage Rule K10.C3 or must they be measured separately under the rules of another work section?

Only those components supplied by the partition manufacturer as part of the proprietary system are deemed included within the measured item for a 'proprietary partition'.

If timber grounds are required to provide support and/or fixings for any item attached to the partition and are not provided as a component, therefore needing to be acquired from a different source, they must be measured separately in accordance with the appropriate work section, as stated in Coverage Rule K10.C3. In the case of timber grounds they would be measured as 'supports' in accordance with the rules of Work Section G20, viz. G20.11, 12 or 13.

# G30 Metal profiled sheet decking

▶ Fire stop filler blocks have to be fitted between the soffit of the ribbed steel deck and the top steel beams. Edge beams require one row of filler blocks, intermediate beams require two rows of filler blocks. Should separate items be measured for the different situations?

Yes, as G30.11.1 and Supplementary Information items G30.S1 to S4 inclusive.

A loose mat insulation quilt is fixed to the underside of profiled metal roof sheeting. In which work section should the quilt be measured?

G30 is for metal decking only, insulating mats should be measured separately under P10.

Holes have to be cut through the profiled sheeting for service pipes. In which section are the holes measured?

Holes in decking must be measured as extra over the decking, G30.3.1.1–2.

Is a concrete slab on permanent metal deck formwork a composite item?

No.

Please clarify how the net area of profiled metal floor decking is calculated.

General Rule 3.1: 'Work shall be measured net as fixed in position except where otherwise stated in a measurement rule applicable to the work'. G30 has no measurement rules varying this rule. The area would be that of the flat plane covered by the profiled deck.

# H Cladding/Covering

## H20 Rigid sheet cladding

## K11 Rigid sheet flooring/sheathing/decking/sarking/ linings/casings

## K13 Rigid sheet fine linings/panelling

How should rigid fire protection boarding around a structural steel member be measured?

It should be measured in accordance with the rules of H20, K11 or K13. The girth will be measured on the external finished face as Measurement Rule M4.

In which section should rigid fire protection board lining around isolated steel columns and beams be measured?

This should be measured as K11.6 and 7. The girth of each face is measured on the external finished face, Measurement Rule K11.M4.

Please define the measurement of rigid sheet linings to sloping ceilings.

MDF lining to the underside of a roof should be measured in $m^2$ as linings to sloping ceilings over 300mm wide (K11.3.1.*.2), incorporating the relevant NBS spec. reference into the description to provide the information required by Supplementary Information items. Polythene vapour barrier is deemed included in the measured item of ceiling linings as Coverage Rule K11.C1(b).

Should rigid mineral fibre batt fire barriers in ceiling voids be measured under Work Section K11 or P10?

These batts can be measured in either work section subject to the provision of Measurement Rule M2 in P10. Given that the calculation of the net area will differ depending on which rules are used, the rate must therefore also differ.

A Bill item for a carpet floor covering contains an NBS reference relating to the specification for the carpet. Within the specification item is a requirement that the carpet must be laid on a sheet of plywood underlay. There is no mention of the plywood in the Bill description. Is the plywood deemed included in the carpet item because of the unique cross reference or should it have been measured separately?

The plywood must be measured separately as rigid sheet flooring in accordance with the rules of Work Section K11.2.

The use of a unique cross reference to a specification clause does not override General Rule 4.2 which does not allow the aggregation of items except as provided by General Rule 9.1 or unless the rules have been clearly qualified.

# H31 Metal profiled/flat sheet cladding/covering

▶ Is raking cutting at hips or valleys in profiled metal sheet roofing deemed included within the measured item for the hip or valley?

No, the cutting is measured in accordance with H31.20.1.

When raking cutting is measured to a hip or valley is it measured once along the centre line or twice along both edges?

The cutting is measured twice.

▶ Is waste deemed included in an item of raking cutting on profiled metal roof sheeting?

Yes, H31.20.1 and General Rule 4.6.

▶ Should the Bill item for a hole through profiled metal roofing include the flashing kit?

No, H31.12 is labour only for forming the hole; H31.18.1–6 is for flashing kits and the like.

▶ Please clarify the measurement of roof light openings in standing seam roofing.

The standing seam roofing and integral rooflights would be measured in accordance with the following rules of SMM7.

- Roof covering as H31.1.1.*.1–2 in m².
- Voids greater than 1m² would be deducted from the overall area of roof covering.
- Voids equal to or less than 1m² would not be deducted from the overall area of roof covering and the work involved in forming this would be deemed included, Coverage Rule C1(a).
- Boundary work as H31.3–17.1.*.1–2 in linear metres. These items are only measured to edges of voids that exceed 1m².
- Rooflights as extra over the roof covering as H31.18.3.1, in Nr.

▶ Precurved sheet roofing – what measurement information is required?

The sheeting will be measured in accordance with H31.1.*.*.1. The Bill description must make reference to the requirement for the sheeting to be passed through a curving machine. Without this information an estimator cannot assess how much sheeting should go through a machine.

# H60 Plain roof tiling

# H61 Fibre cement slating

# H62 Natural slating

# H63 Reconstructed stone slating/tiling

# H64 Timber shingling

# H65 Single lap roof tiling

# H66 Bituminous felt shingling

▶ Valleys in concrete or clay tiled roofs:
- Is the lead valley deemed a boundary?
- In which section of SMM7 is the lead valley lining in a tiled roof measured?

- Yes.
- In H60.9, stating kind, quality and size of materials as required by Supplementary Information item H60.S1.

▶ If the lead valley lining is measured in another work section, must an item for forming a valley still be measured to allow the contractor the opportunity of pricing the work listed in Coverage Rule H60.C2 as 'deemed included'?

Yes.

▶ Should the gap of an open lead lined valley be deducted from total roof area when measuring tiled roof coverings?

Yes, each slope should be measured separately with the edge of the valley forming a boundary.

Should underlay, etc. be deducted if not continued through to eaves or verge?

Yes, General Rules 2.12 and 2.13 require that separate items be measured if the required supplementary information varies.

▶ Please define the measurement of tiling to a valley.

A valley formed by tiles cut to rake would be measured as stated in S5, in accordance with H60.9. Abutments would be measured where tiles abut walls or other structures such as rooflights, chimneys, etc.

▶ If a variation order has been issued by architect to remedy a discrepancy between drawings and Bill items, must the QS remeasure the work in accordance with SMM7?

Yes, General Rule 1.2 states rules apply to both proposed and executed work.

▶ Please define the measurement of concrete roof tiles.

- Roof tiles – H60.1 – m$^2$
- Abutments – H60.3 – m
- Eaves – H60.4 – m
- Verges – H60.5 – m
- Ridges – H60.6 – m
- Hips – H60.7 – m
- Valleys – H60.9 – m
- Fittings; hip irons – H60.10.4 – Nr
- Holes – H60.11 – Nr

▶ In coverage Rule H60.C2, a horizontal line separates Classification 5 Verges from 6 Ridges onwards. Does this mean that boundary work stated in C2 is not included in Classification H60.6–9?

Classification items H60.6–9 are covered by all incidental items listed in Coverage Rules H60.C2.

▶ Please define the measurement of valleys.

The forming of a valley is a measurable item in accordance with H60.9 with the kind, quality and size of material given as Supplementary Information item S1 and the method of forming given as Supplementary Information item S5.

This would apply even if the valley was lined in sheet lead.

An item must be measured somewhere in the BoQ to allow the tenderer the opportunity of pricing those elements of labour or material deemed included in Coverage Rule C2.

▶ Is the cutting of roof tiles at a valley deemed included in the valley item?

No, the edge of tiling against a valley is measured as an 'abutment', as H66.3.*.*.1–2. Cutting is deemed included in this item, Coverage Rule C2.

# H62  Natural slating

▶ How is boundary work to slate roofing measured at abutments and valleys?

In linear metres in accordance with H62.3 and 9 respectively.

If the lead valley in a slate covered pitch roof is measured in a work section other than H62, is the cutting of slates at the valley deemed included in the general item for slate roof covering?

No, for any work associated with an item listed in H62.3 to 9 inclusive to be deemed included an item of boundary work must be measured. An item for the valley must be measured stating that the lead is measured elsewhere.

▶ If the ridge of a slate roof is capped with lead and this is measured in a different work section to the slating, should an item still be measured in the slate section for the 'ridge' in order to allow for cutting, etc. which, in accordance with Coverage Rule H62.C2, is deemed included within the item of ridge?

Yes, for any work associated with an item listed in H62.3–9 inclusive to be deemed included, an item of boundary work must be measured. An item for the 'ridge' must be measured stating that a lead capping is measured elsewhere.

## H63 Reconstructed stone slating/tiling

▶ Please define the measurement information required for reconstructed stone slating.

The various sizes of slates needed to achieve the designed finish (curved) must be included with Bill descriptions and/or preambles if the Bill item is to comply with all the requirements of H63.

## H70 Malleable metal sheet prebonded coverings/cladding

## H71 Lead sheet coverings/flashings

## H72 Aluminium strip/sheet coverings/flashings

## H73 Copper strip/sheet coverings/flashings

## H74 Zinc strip/sheet coverings/flashings

## H75 Stainless steel strip/sheet coverings/flashings

## H76 Fibre bitumen thermoplastic sheet coverings/flashings

▶ At what point does a drip become an upstand?

A drip become an upstand when it exceeds 50mm.

Does an upstand have to be at an abutment or edge of roof or can it be within the body of the sheet roof?

An upstand can be a step within the general area of sheet roof covering.

What 'allowance' is applicable to a 75mm high step in the roof?

1000mm, as the allowances for an upstand and downstand must be made, Measurement Rule H70.M2(f).

The edge of a downstand is finished with a welted edge. Should the welted seam allowance be allowed as well as the allowance for the downstand?

Yes, the allowances are cumulative, see H70.M2 (b) and (f).

Should a 500mm allowance be given for a 100mm turndown at a fascia?

Yes, see H70.M2(f).

▶ How should a drip flashing piece be measured at the eaves of a copper sheet roof?

It should be measured in linear metres with a dimensioned description or diagram. The general area of copper roofing will have included the eaves projection and welted edge allowance.

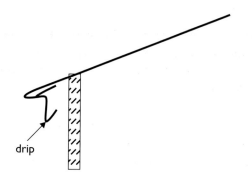

drip

Should a soffit drip formed at the edge of a fascia lining be measured separately?

No, it is included within the girth of the fascia.

Should there be a measured item for forming standing seams in zinc sheet roofing?

Yes, H74 Supplementary Information item S4 applies.

Must the 500mm allowance be automatically made for all upstand/downstands when they occur in sheet roofing?

Yes.

Must the allowances for sheet metal coverings be made?

Yes, allowances for sheet metal coverings listed in H70 Rule M2(a)–(f) are mandatory and must be included in the calculation of area sheet metal covering. The allowances are meant to cover the whole range of sheet metal coverings as H70 to H76 inclusive.

# H71 Lead sheet coverings/flashings

▶ Please clarify the measurement of a tapering gutter?

The total girth of the narrowest section should be added to the total girth of the widest section and then averaged.

▶ Is a contractor entitled to adjust the flashing rate by the number and quantity of preformed bends?

The number of preformed bends must be enumerated within the description of all linear flashings.

▶ Must the full allowance of 500mm be added for a simple upstand when calculating the area of a lead flat roof even if the drawing shows it to be no more than 100mm high?

Yes, the allowances listed in Measurement Rule H71.M2 are mandatory.

▶ Where more than one labour listed in Measurement Rule H71.M2 occurs in the one detail are the allowances cumulative or does the largest allowance cover all labours?

The allowances are cumulative and must be applied for each and every labour that occurs in a detail.

Knowing that these allowances have been made the estimator can decide how much additional sheet metal to allow for when pricing the detail.

▶ How should the 75mm turn down of sheet lead at the change of slope detail of a mansard roof be measured where the sheet lead covered upper sloping roof meets the slate covered lower roof?

This is a dressing. It should be measured in linear metres. The area of metal below the change of slope must be included within the overall area of roof sheeting.

▶ A BoQ measures sheet lead coverings to lead gutters in linear metres, giving the girth and describing various labours. The girths are generally wider than a standard sheet of lead therefore the gutter needs a longitudinal roll. No reference is made to the roll in the BoQ description.

Should a contractor allow for this roll and the additional lead allowance within the rate because, by experience, he should know that lead over a certain width needs to be jointed?

No, General Rule 2.11 states that 'where the coverage rules include materials they should be mentioned in the item description' as required by Supplementary Information item S4.

What allowance should be taken where lead work to a dome turns up at a timber hip piece?

Lead turn up at a hip batten constitutes an upstand. The allowance is 500mm for each upstand.

What allowance should be added to general roof area for underturn and welt at the edge of a roof?

The turn down and welt at the edge of a roof would attract allowances of 500mm and 80mm respectively for downstand and welt.

Where a flat roof has steps/drips within the general area which are 70mm high, what total allowance should be taken per step?

A step within a general area of roof covering which exceeds 50mm high is considered both an upstand and a downstand and would attract 1000mm allowance.

Should allowance for laps and upstands/downstands be added even if a dimension is given on drawing?

Allowances must be made as described in Measurement Rule M2 irrespective of any conflicting drawings. These allowances are over and above the net superficial area.

Please clarify the allowance for each lap in sheet lead.

An allowance of 500mm must be added to the width of sheet lead for each lap within the width as H71.M2(e).

What allowance should be made for rolls in lead sheet which are higher than 50mm?

500mm to each side of the roll, as if for an upstand. It can be left to the discretion of the surveyor how an allowance is made in this circumstance provided the surveyor clearly highlights the qualification to the allowance rules contained in Measurement Rule M2.

Please define the measurement of a dome.

The full allowance for any items listed in H71.M2(a) to (f) inclusive must be included in the gross area when calculating the area of sheet lead covering of a dome. The basic area of lead sheet measured will be the area in contact with base, not the cumulative area of sheets used.

# H72  Aluminium strip/sheet coverings/flashings

▶ In a Russian gutter detail, the subcontractor has measured the girth including allowances. The surveyor has billed the items as gutters and aprons in linear metres. Please advise.

The calculation of the girth of a gutter would be with the net girth being calculated first and then allowances added for each drip, welt, roll, seam, lap and upstand/downstand encountered within that girth.

▶ When does a drip become an upstand?

A drip becomes an upstand and a downstand when it exceeds 50mm in height.

When does an abutment with Kingroll become an upstand?

An abutment with Kingroll becomes an upstand when the roll height exceeds 50mm.

What is a downstand?

A downstand is any 90° turn down on the edge of the sheet metal covering or any step in level of general sheeting which exceeds 50mm in height.

In dormer cheeks – is an allowance of 500mm made when the lead cheek carries over a lead soaker upstand and under timber cladding?

Yes.

# H73  Copper strip/sheet covering/flashings

# H74  Zinc strip/sheet coverings/flashings

▶ How is the beaded edge of zinc sheet roofing measured?

An allowance of 180mm is added to the overall area of zinc work in accordance with H74.M2(a). A linear item for the beaded edge is measured as H74.23.2.

How is zinc sheet roofing to a capped roll measured, as shown on sketch?

cap

What is the correct rule for measuring a one piece zinc sheet covering to a small flat porch roof which contains downturns at edges and an upstand at its abutment with the wall?

What allowances should be made when measuring the following zinc sheet:

1.  the 100mm downstand;
2.  the welted edge;
3.  the upturn below the ridge cap;
4.  the ridge cap.

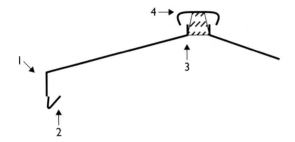

A capping piece is measured in linear metres as H74.14.1 plus the roll allowance of 250mm is added to the general area of zinc to allow for the turn-ups at the batten.

It should be numbered. It is similar to a hatch cover and therefore should be measured as H74.27. All labours, etc. are deemed included. The dimensional description should include allowances.

The allowances would be as set out in Measurement Rule H74.M2 (a) to (f) inclusive. These allowances are mandatory.

1.  The 100mm is added to the general area of roof sheeting and an allowance of 500mm added, M2(f).
2.  An 80mm allowance is added to the general area of roof sheeting, M2(b), and a linear item measured for the welted edge, H74.23.1.
3.  The height of upturn is added to the general area of roof sheeting and an allowance of 500mm added, M2(f).
4.  The ridge cap would be measured in linear metres complete with a dimensioned diagram, H74.14.1–2. All labours needed to form the capping are deemed included, Coverage Rule H74.C2.

# H75  Stainless steel strip/sheet coverings/flashings

The drawings show a sheet stainless steel ridge capping. Should the vertical edges be measured as upstands (therefore attracting the 500mm allowance) or as welted edges?

The area of the vertical upturns of the roof covering would be added to the overall area of the roof covering and the 500mm allowance added.

The ridge cap should be measured in linear metres in accordance with H75.14.1 or 2 with overall dimensions being given in the description or shown on a dimensioned diagram.

Separate linear items should to be measured for forming welted edges to the edges of the ridge cap, as H75.23.1.

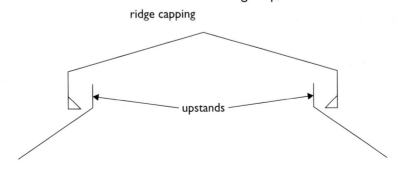

ridge capping

upstands

# J Waterproofing

# J21 Mastic asphalt roofing/insulation/finishes

▶ What is the correct method to calculate the girth of asphalt to a flat roof gutter?

The girth will be the exposed face as Measurement Rule J21.M4, see sketch below.

▶ How are asphalt edge labours measured?

The labour involved in finishing edges of asphalt should be measured in linear metres as J21.13 or 14. Metal flashing, felt and timber ground would be measured separately. All labours on a verge detail would be deemed included in item for fascias measured as J21.6.1–4.*.2.

▶ A mastic asphalt membrane is laid over a plant room floor. Should a deduction in the general area of floor asphalt be made for machine bases, 2000 x 300mm, that are cast off the floor slab?

No, voids less than 1m² are not deducted, Measurement Rule J21.M3.

Should an item be measured for working asphalt into outlet pipes?

No, this is deemed included, Coverage Rule J21.C1(c). The cost of labour and additional materials involved should be ascertained from the drawings that must accompany the BoQ, J21.P1(a)

▶ Please clarify the measurement of insulation in Work Section J21.

Supplementary Information item J21.S1 requires details of underlays to be given in the Bill description. This includes insulation.

This information may be given as a cross reference to a specification item. This complies with General Rule 4.2, which permits information to be given in a Bill description by a precise and unique cross reference.

▶ Is dressing mastic asphalt skirtings around brick vents a measurable item?

Dressing skirtings around brick vents is deemed included in the item for forming skirting, Coverage Rule J21.C4.

Is the dressing of mastic asphalt around copper overflow pipes chargeable?

Dressing asphalt around pipes is deemed included. Forming collars around pipes, etc. is measurable, J21.18.1.

Is dressing mastic asphalt through preformed channels that pass through concrete kerb measurable?

Dressing asphalt through preformed channels is not measurable, Coverage Rule J21.C5. The length of the kerb would be measured overall all channels without deductions.

Are gateway openings through a concrete kerb deductible from linear measurement of the mastic kerb covering?

Gateway openings in asphalt covered concrete kerbs would not be deductible if the covering is continuous across the openings.

Mastic asphalt capping to the top of the concrete kerb has a bullnose edge. Is preforming these edges measurable?

Edges and arises on asphalt coverings to kerbs are deemed included within the item of covering to kerbs, Coverage Rule J21.C5.

# J40 Flexible sheet tanking/damp proofing

# J42 Single layer polymeric roof coverings

Is 'fully lapping and bonding the edge of a floor damp-proof membrane to the projecting edge of the wall damp-proof course' a measurable item?

Yes, this is boundary work, it should be measured as J40.4.2 and includes everything described in Coverage Rule J40.C2.

Should site testing of the membrane be priced within measured items?

Testing of completed work which is not left to the discretion of the contractor would be a measurable item.

Part of the single layer roofing has to be applied to a vertical surface that is within the general body of the roof. It is 900mm high. Should this work be measured in m² as roof covering to a vertical pitch in accordance with J42.2.1, or should it be measured in linear metres in accordance with J42.4–15, with the girth stated in 200mm increments?

Vertical coverings should be measured and described as having a pitch of 90°.

Please define the method of measurement for roof ballast.

The ballast laid on top of a roof covering is included within the roof covering item, J42.2.1, and therefore is measured in m² with the thickness of the ballast given in the Bill description.

# K Linings/Sheathing/Dry partitioning

## Important note

All references now relate to SMM7 revised 1998, incorporating amendments 1 and 2 (2000).

## K10 Plasterboard dry linings/partitions/ceilings

▶ Please define the measurement of plasterboard dry linings to walls.

These are measured in linear metres as K10.2.1.1, stating the height in stages of 300mm.

▶ The plasterboard facing of a partition is shown on the drawings to continue 100mm upwards past the ceiling line. Should this area of plasterboard be included in the measurement?

Yes, the height of the plasterboard has not been left to the discretion of the contractor.

▶ New proprietary metal stud plasterboard lined partitions are to be erected inside an existing room. The partitions are to be erected around existing service pipes. Should this work be described as 'obstructed by integral services' as required by rule K10.1.*.*.3?

No, integral services in this context refers to new services that must be installed within the new partitions. Reference to the integral services allows the contractor the opportunity of pricing the coordination that the contractor needs to provide between different trades.

The existence of existing services must be shown in the drawings or description of the works.

▶ Dry lining has been described in spec. section K10 but measured in Work Section M. Is this correct?

One would expect the work to have been measured in the same work section as specified. It should preferably be measured in Work Section K10.

▶ A Bill item reads 'Taping to internal partitions, Spec. K31:110'. Part of this spec. item K31:110 refers to a subspec. item that includes reference to a finish application to be applied to the entire surface area of the partitions.

Should this surface treatment be measured separately?

No, this must be stated in the description.

▶ Should dry linings to 'short walls' with narrow returns each end be measured as a three-sided column?

No:
- the dry lining to the face is measured in linear metres as K10.2.1.1;
- the lining to reveals is measured in linear metres as K10.2.4.1.

▶ How are holes for pipes through plasterboard faced metal stud partitions measured?

They are enumerated as P31.20.2.

▶ Must the Bill description of a proprietary partition make reference to all components or can reference be made to a trade name or a catalogue reference?

All components that are part of a proprietary system are deemed included in a Bill item as required by Coverage Rule K10.C3.

▶ Is trimming to openings included in the measurement of fair ends when measuring plasterboard partitions in accordance with the rules of Work Section K10?

Yes, as stated in Measurement Rule K10.M12.

▶ Should the item of angles in dry lined partitions include both the internal and external angle or should two items be measured?

Only one item should be measured, K10.3. The item of angles in partitions includes both the internal and external angle face.

Where should the passing through partitions of conduits not exceeding 55mm be measured for:

(a) electrical conduit?

(b) mechanical conduit?

(c) other conduit?

These are measured in accordance with P31.20.2.1.2 except where the conduit is part of an electrical installation where individual holes are not measured, but an overall item is measured for the work in accordance with P31.19.1.\*.\*.

▶ Would the following situations of double-sided partitions running past a concrete beam be classified as the scenario described in Measurement Rule K10.M10?

A degree of flexibility is needed when measuring partitions that are design to coordinate with structural dimensions.

Diagram 1 – one face of a double-sided partition is carried across the surface of the beam.

Yes, the partition height is measured overall to the soffit of the structural slab with no item measured for an abutment.

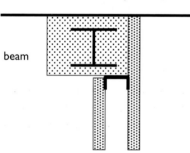

beam

Diagram 2 – due to construction vagaries some partitions have one face offset from the obstruction therefore requiring a separate fixing method, i.e. a separate metal support system.

No, the partition again would be measured full height to the soffit of the structural slab with no item being measured for an abutment.

Should an 'extra over' item (or separate item) be measured?

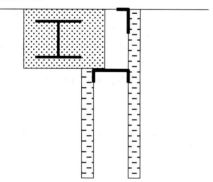

▶ Should an item be measured in the BoQ for forming a door opening in a proprietary dry lined partition?

Not unless the void extends full height, K10.M8.

▶ A door opening in a proprietary metal stud partition is trimmed with metal channels. Are these trimmers measurable?

No, see Coverage Rule K10.C3(b).

Timber subframes are set into the channel trimmers. Are they measurable?

Yes, as butt jointed supports, G20.11.

The proprietary partition is set on a timber sole plate that is not part of the system. Is it measurable?

Yes, as plates, G20.8.

The proprietary partition system is specified to have a deflection head. How is this measured and described?

Provided relevant drawings and spec. showing the deflection head detail have accompanied the BoQ, there is no need to measure a separate item for the deflection head. It is part of the proprietary system and deemed included in the BoQ item for the partition, Coverage Rule K10.C3. Separate items should be measured in the BoQ for partitions with and without deflection heads.

▶ What deductions for door openings should be made from proprietary partitions that have been measured in linear metres, stating their height in accordance with K10.1.1?

Deductions are only made for openings that extend the full height of the partition, Measurement Rule K10.M8.

▶ To which openings should one measure fair ends and trimming openings?

Fair ends are only measured where the exposed end of the partition is finished with the same finish as its face, Measurement Rule K10.M12. This applies to any fair end even if the opening which it lines has not been subject to deduction.

Trimming of the opening is included in the fair end item, Definition Rule K10.D6.

▶ Please clarify what 'full width' and 'full girth' refer to in Definition Rule K10. D5.

This occurs when the width or girth of the opening is exactly the same as the partition in which the opening exists.

▶ A description gives working height of 6600–6900mm but the head channel was fixed to an elliptical shaped steel roof beam, involving curved cutting. How should the description of the metal stud partition read?

Separate linear items should be measured for each height stage where the partition height increases due to a curved or sloping soffit. The description of the partition must include reference to the shape of the underside of the steel beam.

▶ Please define the measurement of plasterboard partitions.

They are measured in linear metres as K10.1.1.2.

# SMM7 Q & A

▶ Would the tenderer be expected to include for items such as DPM, acoustic sealant and mastic sealant within a metal stud plasterboard partition?

If damp-proof membrane, acoustic sealant or mastic sealant items are standard components they would be deemed as included within the rates for partitions and ancillary items such as abutments.

If they are not standard components they must be measured separately in accordance with their relevant work sections.

▶ Under K10.10 (fixings for heaving fittings), should the nogging (150mm x 100mm timber) be numbered or should the item it is supporting be numbered, i.e. one radiator needs four noggings, therefore, should the BoQ item state one or four number?

Fixings for heavy fittings are enumerated as per the item to be supported, i.e. radiators, leaving the number of noggings to the discretion of the contractor. See Coverage Rule K10.C8.

▶ Would IPS (Integrated Plumbing Systems) panels for sanitary ware be classed as access panels under K10.11?

IPS panels would not be classed as access panels under K10.11. They should be measured separately in Work Section N13.4.1.1.

▶ How is measurement of deflection head in proprietary partitions dealt with?

This should be included in the description of the item.

▶ Plasterboard partitions/linings:

Please define the measurement of:
- mastic and acoustic strips,
- door openings, and
- channel trims.

Acoustic sealants and intumescent mastic strips, where not part of a proprietary partition system, should be measured separately in linear metres.

The number of door openings to be formed in partitions must be assessed from information accompanying the BoQ. Fair ends are only measured where they are constructed as K10.M12 and this applies equally to ends exposed by trimming openings.

Channel trim to the edge of a plasterboard suspended ceiling should be measured in linear metres.

▶ If timber grounds are shown in a manufacturer's installation guide or the drawn details of a proprietary partition system, are they deemed included as a component of a proprietary partition system as required by Coverage Rule K10.C3 or must they be measured separately under the rules of another work section?

Only those components supplied by the partition manufacturer as part of the proprietary system are deemed included within the measured item for a 'proprietary partition'.

If timber grounds are required to provide support and/or fixings for any item attached to the partition and are not provided as a component, therefore needing to be acquired from a different source, they must be measured separately in accordance with the appropriate work section, as stated in Coverage Rule K10.C3. In the case of timber grounds they would be measured as 'supports' in accordance with the rules of Work Section G20, viz. G20.11, 12 or 13.

▶ Please define the measurement for BWIC in relation to cutting or forming partition holes.

Cutting or forming holes for mechanical and electrical services, pipes, conduits, etc. are measurable items and should be measured under P31.19–26 inclusive.

# K30 Panel partitions

▶ Should openings in proprietary partitions formed from integral fittings be deducted?

No, they are measured 'extra over'.

▶ Do the items of partitioning measured in accordance with Work Section K30 include the responsibility for design?

No, General Rule 4.6 sets out what is normally deemed included within all measured items.

Any work in which design is required must be specifically described as 'Contractor Designed'.

# K40 Demountable suspended ceilings

▶ A new suspended ceiling is installed in a room in an existing building. Should an item of 'bonding/jointing new to existing' be measured in accordance with the Additional Rules item 1.1 where the new ceiling abuts the existing walls?

No, the Additional Rules item would only be measured where an existing suspended ceiling was being extended.

In this case the normal edge detail would be measured in accordance with K40.8 and all work would be described as being in an existing building in accordance with General Rule 13.

▶ A suspended ceiling has an edge detail that comprises a different type of tile than that of the main ceiling. The two types of tile are separated by an angle piece. How should this edge detail of the suspended ceiling be measured?

The border tile is measured in linear metres in accordance with K40.3.1–3.1–2.

The inner angle piece is a floating trim and measured as K40.8.2, and the outer plain trim as K40.8.1.

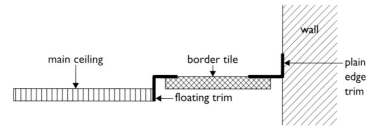

▶ How is the forming of slots for air conditioning grills in suspended ceiling panels measured?

Cutting or forming holes, etc. must be measured in accordance with P31.20.1.

Can the forming of these slots be deemed included in the overall item for suspended ceilings if shown on the drawings that accompany the BoQ?

No.

▶ A suspended ceiling system is suspended from an intermediate framework of steel channel sections.

No, the suspension system referred to in K40.C1(b) refers to members which are an integral part of the ceiling system.

Should this framework of steel channels be held to be included within the Bill item for the suspended ceiling system, even though the specification states that the suspended system is to include all 'carriers, hangers, main runners and primary channels'?

The channel sections referred to would be considered to be structural members and measured separately.

# SMM7 Q & A

▶ How are steps in a plasterboard lined suspended ceiling measured – as 'bulkheads' or 'upstands'?

They are measured as upstands, as K40.5.1.1–2.

▶ How wide must an isolated strip be before it is measured in m²?

Isolated strips are always measured in linear metres, K40.3.

An isolated strip is measured when the strip is narrower than the specified lining unit dimension, Definition Rule K40.D3, except where the strip lies between the boundary and the first line of integral fittings (i.e. the suspension system) as stated in Measurement Rule K40.M7.

▶ Should a suspended ceiling be measured over or between continuous strips of service housings (i.e. recessed light fitting/linear slot vents)?

If the service housings are not integral with the suspended ceiling, the ceiling would be measured up to the edges of the service housings.

▶ How should the service housings be measured if they are not integral with the ceiling system?

They should be measured in linear metres as fittings, K40.13.

▶ Suspended ceilings – please define the term 'isolated strip' when referring to a suspended plasterboard ceiling.

An isolated strip is that which is narrower than the specified width of the plasterboard sheet. If a ceiling is lined with standard 2400 x 1200mm plasterboard sheets then an isolated strip is any strip less than 1200mm wide. If ceiling is to be lined with 600mm wide plasterboard planks then an isolated strip is a strip less than 600mm wide.

▶ If a floating trim requires bracing to prevent lateral movement, is this bracing measurable?

No, all support work to trims is deemed included, Coverage Rule K40.C1(b).

▶ Are MF6 edge trims to MF and Gypliner ceilings a measurable item?

Yes, the perimeter channel would be measured in linear metres in accordance with K40.8.1.1, i.e. plain edge trims.

▶ Where an MF plasterboard suspended ceiling abuts a full height plasterboard partition, is there a separate measurable item or is the work included in the ceiling item?

An item of 'plain edge trim' should be measured where the MF ceiling abuts a full height partition. There would be no measurable items in the partition work section.

▶ How do you measure curved areas of suspended ceilings?

See K40.1.1–3.1.3.

▶ Should the area of edge trims be deducted from the area of a suspended ceiling when calculating the ceiling area?

No.

▶ Should concealed perimeter angles/trims for a plasterboard suspended ceiling be measured?

Yes.

▶ Should the area of light fittings and ceiling heating panels be deducted from the area of suspended ceilings upon remeasuring?

Yes, but the ceiling description should refer to integral fittings and drawings should accompany the Bills to show the extent of integral fittings.

▶ The BoQ description for a suspended ceiling made no reference to services within the ceiling void. There were extensive services necessitating secondary gridwork.

Should the work be remeasured to allow for the necessary changes in construction?

The BoQ description should make reference to the scope and location of integral fittings, the extent of services located in the void and suspension systems obstructed by services. If any of the above information is missing the work should be remeasured.

▶ Please clarify Rule D3 of Work Section K40 *Demountable suspended ceilings*, relating to isolated strips of ceilings.

Rule K40.D3 defines an 'isolated strip' as being 'a strip of ceiling narrower than the specified relevant lining unit dimension'.

▶ Is a heated radiant panel an integral fitting?

A radiant ceiling panel is not an integral fitting if it does not rely on the ceiling's suspension system to provide support.

▶ If a radiant ceiling panel is not an integral fitting should its area be deducted from that of the adjacent suspended ceiling?

A radiant ceiling panel that is not an integral fitting would be deducted when calculating the area of suspended ceiling.

# L  Windows/Doors/Stairs

## L10  Windows/Rooflights/Screens/Louvres

A glazed softwood screen is measured in the BoQ as '500 x 2600mm glazed screen; fixing with screws; Georgian wired glass; panes 600 x 600mm; As NBS Spec. Ref. L10.510'. No drawing is referred to and no frame size or section is identified. Would the Bill item description be assumed to include trims such as architraves if not part of the component?

No, only items listed in Coverage Rule L10.C2 are deemed included.

The Bill descriptions for replacement metal windows made no reference to flat mild steel mullions but they are shown on the drawings that are referred to in the Bill description. These steel mullions are not an integral part of the window system. Are they deemed included?

No, Coverage Rules L11.C1, C2 and C3 identify what is deemed included. The mild steel mullions are not an integral part of the windows and therefore should be measured separately.

## L20  Doors/Shutters/Hatches

Doors are described in the BoQ as double swing but make no reference to rounded meeting stiles. Should these edges be assumed included?

No, the shape would be deemed square unless otherwise described. If different the shape of the meeting stile must be given in the Bill description, drawing, Bill diagram or the relevant specification clauses.

The BoQ description of a set of sliding/folding doors gives the overall size but does not state the number of leaves. Should the number and size of leaves be stated in Bill description?

Yes, unless they are left to the discretion of the contractor.

Plywood packing pieces are shown on the drawings behind door frames. Are they deemed included with the Bill items for the frames?

No, they would be measured as 'butt jointed supports' in accordance with G20.11.2.

Please define a door set.
- Are doors pre-hung?
- Does a set include architraves?
- Does a set include ironmongery?

Door sets are treated as composite items (including architraves and, if fully specified, ironmongery) and hanging doors is deemed included (Measurement Rule L20.M4 and Coverage Rule L20.C1).

Should the decoration of joinery items that require finishing off site be measured separately from the joinery item and measured in Work Section M60?

No, the off site surface treatments applied as part of the manufacturing process should be measured with the component as Supplementary Information item L20.S3.

If relevant information is not given in the BoQ description, whether as part of the worded description, by a unique cross reference or by a drawing reference, does this constitute a Bill error?

Yes, General Rules 2 and 4 set out what minimum information must be given when composing Bill descriptions.

# L40 General glazing

▶ A drawing shows a stainless steel canopy that contains laminated glazed panels. How should the glass panels be measured?

These should be measured by enumerating each pane and referring to the drawings in accordance with L40.3.1.1.1–10.

▶ When measuring glazing, should the dimensions of the opening be used or the dimensions of the actual glass?

The dimensions of the opening are used to calculate the area of glass when measuring glazing.

▶ Should 'Solar Control' film to window glass be measured in Work Section P10?

No, it should be measured in Work Section L40 under the rules for 'Special glass' L40.3.1.

# M Surface finishes

## M10 Cement: sand/Concrete screeds/toppings

## M12 Trowelled bitumen/resin/rubber-latex flooring

## M13 Calcium sulfate based screeds

## M20 Plastered/Rendered/Roughcast coatings

## M23 Resin bound mineral coatings

## J10 Specialist waterproof rendering

▶ The BoQ description for sheet vinyl flooring refers to an NBS Specification Reference. This specification item states that concrete subfloors must be prepared with a 'latex levelling screed' and that timber floors must have an underlay of '6mm thick plywood sheeting'. Are these preparation items deemed included in the item of sheet vinyl?

Not unless the rules have been qualified. General Rule 4.1 does not allow the aggregation of a number of measured items that are otherwise required to be measured separately.

▶ An NBS Specification for floor screed includes reference to a board insulation underlay. No mention of this insulation is made in the Bill item. Is this insulation deemed included in the floor screed item?

No, it should be measured separately as M10.24.2. General Rule 4.1 does not allow the aggregation of a number of measured items that are otherwise required to be measured separately.

▶ Why do the rules of Work Section M20 not include separate rules for the measurement of wall plaster to heights above 3.5m?

The BoQ must be accompanied by drawings which show the scope and location of work. From these drawings, the estimator is able to assess the extent of walls which are higher than 3.5m. The decision not to categorise walls by heights was made by the Committee with the full assistance and agreement of representatives from the Plasterers' Trade Association.

▶ Should an item of formwork be measured to the abutting edges of floor screeds of different thicknesses?

Formwork is not measured to edge of a screed. It is classified as 'temporary rules'.

Should an item be measured if there is a rebate at the edge of the screed?

The forming of a rebate in the exposed edge of a screed would not be measured. The rebate is equivalent to a recess or shaped insert as listed in Coverage Rule M10.C1(b).

# SMM7 Q & A

▶ A trowelled cement screed finish was applied to a balcony soffit and exposed edges. The edge is 150mm high. Should narrow faces not exceeding 150mm be measured as bands not exceeding 150mm?

Yes, any trowel applied finish should be measured in accordance with M10, M12, M20, M23 and J10. Work to faces less than 300mm wide is measured in linear metres as work width equal to or less than 300mm in accordance with M10.2.2.1 and Measurement Rule M6.

▶ Should latex levelling screed to the surface of a cement/sand screed be deemed included in the item for that screed?

Not if the provision of a levelling screed is not left to the discretion of the contractor. It must be measured in accordance with Work Section M12.

▶ A Bill item for sheet vinyl floor covering contains an NBS reference relating to the specification for the vinyl. Within the specification item is a requirement that a latex levelling screed must be applied to the concrete subfloor before the vinyl is laid. There is no specific mention of the latex in the Bill description. Is it deemed included in the sheet vinyl item because of the unique cross reference or should it have been measured separately?

The latex levelling compound must be measured separately in accordance with M12.5.1–3.1–4.

The use of a unique cross reference to a specification clause does not override General Rule 4.2 which does not allow the aggregation of items except as provided by General Rule 9.1 or unless the rules of SMM7 have been clearly qualified.

▶ Does Coverage Rule M20.C1(b) mean that the filling of service chases is deemed included within the general measurement of wall plaster?

No, filling chases would be included as 'making good' within the description of the builder's work items measured in Work Section P31.

▶ Metal stop beads have been used to set out the plasterwork. Should these beads be measured separately from other stop beads and described accordingly?

No, it is left to the discretion of the contractor what is used to set out the plasterwork.

▶ Should softwood grounds be measured when used to 'set out' plastering?

No, these are temporary work items used at the discretion of the contractor and therefore not measurable.

▶ Existing precast concrete panels with 12mm wide joints between each panel are to be treated with a thin render. The render is not to be applied to the joints. Is this patterned work?

Yes – defined as patterned work M20.1.1.1.1, see Clause C2 on page 34 of the *Measurement Code*.

▶ Should plasterwork to reveals of windows and other openings be aggregated into the areas of general wall plaster or measured separately?

The work is measured as work to walls. If the reveal is over 300mm wide on face, the area is added to the work to walls that exceeds 300mm in width, M20.1.1.1. If the reveal is 300mm or less in width, the work shall be measured in linear metres as M20.1.2.1.

▶ Should plasterboard that is subsequently to be coated with plaster be measured in accordance with the rules of Work Section K10?

No, plasterboard and its subsequent plaster coatings are measured in accordance with M20.1–4.1–2.2, Coverage Rule M20.C3 and Supplementary Information item M20.S1. Only proprietary dry lined plasterboard partitions and linings are measured in Work Section K10.

▶ Please define the measurement of plaster coatings to different backgrounds.

General Rule 2.13 requires separate items to be measured for work that is to be applied to different backgrounds or bases.

▶ Should a purpose-made circular arch former be measured separately or should it be grouped within a standard item of plaster edge beads?

Definition Rule M20.D8 states that the 'function of beads as angle beads, casing beads and the like are stated' in the Bill description. An arch former should be described as such and measured separately from plain beads, nosings and the like.

▶ Should plasterwork to walls that exceed 3.50m above floor level be described stating the height in further 1.50m stages?

No, the rules of Work Section M20 do not require plasterwork to walls that exceed 3.50m above floor to be measured separately.

M20.M4 refers only to work to ceilings and beams.

The BoQ must be accompanied by, and read in conjunction with, drawings that show the scope and location of work.

If necessary, the Bill descriptions can be qualified to take account of any unusual or special situation(s), such as a section of wall that, say, has a starting height of 5m above floor level, in accordance with the requirement of General Rule 1.1.

▶ How should the application of a coat of render finish to a wall consisting of large precast concrete panels, each separated by a 12mm joint, be measured?

It should be measured as patterned work in accordance with M20.1.1.1.1. Drawings must accompany the Bills to illustrate the pattern. In Clause C2 on page 34 of the *Measurement Code* it describes patterned work as 'isolated panels within a general wall'.

▶ The specification for plasterboard to ceilings states that all cut or unbound edges must be fully supported by additional timber noggings. How should these noggings be measured?

The rules of Work Section M20 do not include for the measurement of timber grounds, battens or noggings even though they are mentioned within NBS standard specification for Work Section M20. Timber grounds, battens or noggings to receive plasterboard must be measured separately in accordance with the various measurement rules of Work Section G20, as supports in accordance with G20.13.*.1.1–5.

▶ The plasterer has plastered a wall and the plaster finishes approximately 300mm above the level of the suspended ceiling. Are we entitled to payment for the plaster that is above the suspended ceiling level?

The area of plaster to be remeasured is that in contact with the base, Measurement Rule M20.M2. How far the plaster is measured past the suspended ceiling level depends on what is shown on drawn details or given in the specification. It is usual to allow some leeway in order to provide a secure fixing for the edge trim.

▶ Is the following description measured correctly?

'Plasterboard fixed to and including metal firrings, finished with a skim finish'. The firrings are fixed to either existing brick walls or new blockwork walls.

The system should be measured in accordance with the rules of Work Section M20. The metal firrings must be included within the overall Bill description for the plasterboard and plaster as 'work to be carried out prior to fixing of frames or linings' as Supplementary Information item M20.S7.

An alternative way to measure the firrings would be in linear metres as accessories in accordance with M20.24.

▶ A trowelled finish is applied to the soffit and outer edge of a balcony. The outer edge is 200mm wide. Should the work to the soffit and outer edge be girthed together and measured in m² or should the outer edge be measured separately in linear metres?

It should be measured in linear metres as work to narrow widths in accordance with M20.2.2.1 and Measurement Rule M20.M6.

# M21 Insulation with rendered finish

▶ A Bill item for a proprietary insulated render system and its associated specification item makes specific reference to the system's catalogue for what preparatory work is required to the background surface. This catalogue was not attached to the tender documents. Can these preparatory works be deemed included in the Bill description?

Yes, in accordance with General Rule 6.1, a precise and unique cross reference to a catalogue may be given in a Bill description instead of the description required by General Rules 2.6 and 2.12.

Any preparatory work not specified in the manufacturer's catalogue must however be measured elsewhere in the BoQ.

▶ Is the thickness of an insulated panel taken into account when calculating the 'area in contact with the base' where the material overlaps an external corner?

No, Measurement Rule M21.M3 states that 'The area measured is that in contact with the base'.

The traditional interpretation of the base is the existing substrata of brickwork, studwork or the like. Any overlapping of edges of the insulation at external angles is deemed included within the work as stated in Coverage Rule C1(c), provided the tender information includes drawings to show the full scope and location of the work as required by Clause P1 of Work Section M21.

# M30  Metal mesh lathing/Anchored reinforcement for plastered coatings

▶ Tender details inform the tenderer that metal lath suspended ceilings with a plaster finish will have integral light fittings, air diffusers and the like set flush into the ceiling. Can the tenderer assume when pricing the BoQ that the fittings will be installed prior to the plaster finish being applied?

No, the order of work is left to the discretion of the contractor unless stated otherwise in the tender documents.

When components such as light fittings, air diffusers or the like are not to be installed into a suspended metal lath ceiling until after the plasterwork is complete should items be measured for temporary grounds or profile pieces?

No, temporary grounds, laths, beads or the like used to set out openings to receive light fittings are not measurable.

Attendance work in connection with the fittings must be measured in accordance with the rules of Work Section P31.

The BoQ includes 'extra over' items for forming openings for light fittings and the like in the suspended metal lath ceiling. Does this mean that the openings must be formed during the construction process?

No, 'extra over' Bill items for forming openings for light fittings means openings may be formed during the construction process or cut out afterwards.

# M40  Stone/Concrete/Quarry/Ceramic tiling/Mosaic

▶ How should internal and external angles on ceramic tiled skirtings be measured?

If the angles are to be formed by cutting they are not measurable but are deemed included within the item for skirtings. See Coverage Rules C1(d) and C8.

If the angles are formed with special pre-made pieces they are measured as 'corner pieces' or 'special tiles' in accordance with M40.14.*.1 or M40.15.1.2 and Definition Rule M40.D8.

▶ The lane markings on the bottom of a swimming pool are formed in tiles of the same type and quality as the main area of tiling but of a different colour. How should these lane marking tiles be measured?

They should be measured in linear metres as 'extra over' the main type of tiling, stating the width of the band and giving the colour or tile reference.

When measuring tiled treads in accordance with M40.6.*.1 do end tiles have to be measured?

Ends are deemed included as part of a fair edge if formed with a standard tile as stated in Coverage Rule M40.C4. Ends formed with a special tile would be measured and enumerated as 'extra over the work they occur in' in accordance with M40.15.1.1 or 2.

► Should small isolated areas of wall tiling be so described in the BoQ description (i.e. splashbacks)?

There are no specific requirements in the rules except that the drawings or the general description of the work should contain this information. If there is an abnormally high proportion of small isolated areas rather than general areas of tiling it would prudent to expand the Bill description to indicate this fact in accordance with General Rule 1.1.

► Should wall tiling which contains tiles of different colours, but obtained from the same price band, be so described?

The tiling must be described as 'patterned' as required by M40.1.1.*.1. The detail of the pattern must be described or shown by reference to drawings.

► A tile is described and measured as a tread. In accordance with M40.6 are the formation of internal and external angles to such treads deemed included within the measured item? (These angles were formed by the cutting of standard length tiles on site.)

Formation of internal and external angles would be deemed included within the measured item as stated in Coverage Rule M40.C4.

► A mitred angle is formed in a linear run of a 'special' tread tile by on-site cutting. Can the formation of this mitred tile be classified as a 'special' tile under M40.15.1, even though it was not purchased as a pre-made angle tile?

No, the formation of mitred angles by cutting cannot be measured as 'special tiles'. Work to treads, etc. is deemed to include forming angles. See Coverage Rule M40.C4.

► From which position is the girth of an edge tile around a pool assessed?

The girth of an edge tile would be measured along the centre line of the tile.

► The strip of wall above a sink is tiled with one tile 150mm wide up to a window sill that is also tiled with the same tiles to a width of 200mm. Should this tiling be measured overall in m² or measured as two lengths of tiling each not exceeding 300mm wide.

The splashback and sill are both less than 300mm wide and are measured in linear metres. The width of tiling to be measured is 'the width of each face', see Measurement Rule M40.M5.

A wall is covered in wall tiles. A window reveal, 200mm wide, is tiled with the same type of tile. Should this tiling be included in the general area of wall tiling exceeding 300mm wide?

No, reveals to a projection less than 300mm wide would be measured in linear metres as work not exceeding 300mm wide and would not be 'lumped in' with general tiling over 300mm wide.

The width of tiling to be measured is 'the width of each face', see Measurement Rule M40.M5.

► What is the definition of a 'non-standard tile' or 'special tile'?

As well as Definition Rule M40.D8, the Standing Joint Committee would define a 'non-standard' tile as:

(a) a tile or fitting that is not readily available off the shelf; or

(b) does not have a catalogue reference number; or

(c) has to be specially made for the project.

▶ Measurement Rule M40.M1 states that 'work is measured on the exposed face'. Should the area of tiling that lies behind a skirting or above a suspended ceiling be included in the measurement of wall?

Yes, if it is a requirement of the specification or is clearly shown on the drawings. The exposed face in this context is the visible surface before being subsequently hidden by a following trade.

# M41  Terrazzo tiling/In situ terrazzo

▶ A concrete plinth is faced with precast terrazzo. The terrazzo is returned at the end of the plinth to form a trapezium shaped end. How should these end pieces be measured?

These are similar to corner pieces, therefore can be enumerated in accordance with M40.14.1. or they can be measured as extra over the work in which they occur as in M40.15.1–3.

# M50  Rubber/Plastics/Cork/Lino/Carpet tiling/Sheeting

▶ Can latex levelling screed be deemed included in the measured item of a vinyl or carpet floor finish?

The NBS spec. reference included reference to a levelling screed being laid prior to the sheet vinyl flooring.

Yes, if it is left to the discretion of the contractor.

No, if it is a specific requirement of the specification not left to the contractor's discretion. In this case the latex screed must be measured separately in accordance with M12.5.1–3.1–4.

▶ Sheet vinyl flooring has been laid and dressed up the face of a wall over a 'cove former' to form a skirting. Should a separate item be measured where the vinyl floor finish has been dressed up the wall over the cove former?

Yes, a separate item for skirting should be measured in accordance with M50.10.*.1.1–5.

Reference must also be made to the 'cove former' within the description to ensure that it is included within this item.

# M52  Decorative papers/Fabrics

▶ The upper part of a wall is to be hung with one type of wallpaper and the lower part, the dado, to be hung with a different type. The join to be covered with a horizontal dado strip.

Should there be a special item measured for hanging two types of paper on the one wall?

There is no measurement rule in M52 to cover application of two types of paper on one wall. Each type of paper is measured separately as M52.1.1–2. The fact that there are two types of paper to be hung on one wall will be seen on location drawings that must accompany the Bills of quantities.

How is the dado strip measured?

It is measured in linear metres as border strips, M52.3.

# M60 Painting/Clear finishing

▶ How should the painting of a post and rail fence, covered with vertical pales, set with a 20mm gap between each pale, be measured?

Fencing with 20mm gaps between palings should be described as 'plain open type' as M60.D10 and painted in accordance with M60.7.1.1–3. Measurement Rule M60.M10 states that 'plain open type fencing and gates are classified according to the size of their individual members'. Paint to each member shall be measured either in m² or linear metres depending on whether its girth is greater or less than 300mm.

▶ Should the description of painting on timber panelling refer to:
● the ribbed surface?
● panels to be painted in different colours?

Yes, descriptions should refer to:
● irregular surfaces, M60.D4; and
● multi-colour work, M60.D3.

▶ Why do rules for painting not allow for height stages for work to walls?

Because the measured items for forming the ceilings allow for the height stages, they give the information to the contractor. Drawn information must also be provided with the BoQ. All relevant information must then be made available to the painting subcontractor.

▶ Should painting to a scraped finish render be described as to 'irregular surfaces'?

No, this is not an irregular surface as defined in Definition Rule M60.D4. The Bill description must describe the exact nature of the base as required by Supplementary Information item M60.S2 with differing types of base identified separately as required by General Rule 8.2.

▶ Should painting be measured behind skirtings or above suspended ceilings?

It should only be measured if it is a requirement of the specification or drawings.

▶ Should the painting of panelled doors be described as 'painting irregular surfaces'?

Yes, in accordance with M60.1.*.1.3 and Definition Rule D4.

▶ How is painting to vertical close boarded timber palisade fencing measured?

It is measured as close type fencing in m² in accordance with M60.7.2. Allowance must be made for the additional girth of posts and rails as required by Measurement Rule M60.M2.

▶ How is painting a door frame measured if part of the frame is prefinished?

It is measured as two separate girths with the outer piece measured as isolated surfaces.

▶ What girth is measured for timber being primed before fixing? Are there two items measured for each side?

The girth will be the surface that is covered and, if both sides are primed before fixing, the measurement will be the complete girth of the piece of timber and the work described accordingly as M60.1.*.1–3.4 or 5.

▶ Two steel angles are welded together back to back and are finished on site with a gloss paint. Would there be two items of painting measured for each member?

No.

▶ If pre-primed steel is erected on site using unprimed bolts would the priming of the bolts be measured separately from the finishing paintwork?

Yes, the surfaces being painted differ, Supplementary Information item M60.S2.

▶ Should a separate item be measured for the painting of a type of fence not listed in Definition Rule M60.D10 from the painting to those types listed?

No, the types of fencing listed as examples of plain open type fencing in Definition Rule M60. D10 are not exhaustive, therefore just because a particular type is not mentioned it does not preclude it from being described as such.

▶ What is the exact definition of 'a plain open type fence' as described in Definition Rule M60.D10?

Note that SMM7 does not define a tolerance for when a close boarded fence becomes an open boarded fence. However, as a general rule of thumb, any fence that contains gaps between the boards should be considered a plain open type fence.

This allows for the full girth of painting to be measured and the extra labour, if any, in painting edges to be taken into account by the estimator.

The types of fencing listed as examples of plain open type fencing in Definition Rule D10 are not exhaustive, therefore just because a particular type is not mentioned it does not preclude it from being described as such.

▶ Assuming that the same type of paint is to be applied to the same type of background should drawings be provided with the Bills of quantities to allow the estimator the opportunity of seeing the different degrees of complexity when pricing the painting to different types of ornamental fencing?

Yes, if there are significant differences, then, in accordance with General Rule 1.1, drawings would provide the necessary more detailed information.

▶ How is painting of glazed window and screens with opening centre hung sashes measured?

It is measured in accordance with M60.2.1–4.1–3.1–6. The area is measured flat to each side between reveals, Measurement Rule M60.M5. Painting is to be separated into internal and external as Definition Rule D1.

See sketch below.

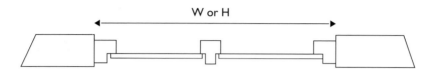

W or H

▶ How should 'painting tongued and grooved wall boarding on site prior to fixing' be measured?

It should be measured in accordance with M60.1.*.1–3.4.

The girth referred to in the Bill description must be the girth of each individual board and not that of the fixed boarding, as defined in Measurement Rule M60.M2.

▶ How does one measure painting to timber that is described in the specification 'to be applied to hidden surfaces'?

The Bill item should state that the painting is to be carried out prior to fixing, either on site or off site, depending on the type of item to be painted.

▶ Should painting the surfaces of wrot and sawn timber be separately measured?

Yes, Supplementary Information item M60.S2 requires the nature of the base be given in the Bill description.

▶ Should painting to a 'peep proof' fence be measured 4 times instead of 'both faces' as per following plan sketch?

Plan of peep proof fence: vertical boards fixed alternately to each side of rail.

No, the fencing sketched would be considered to be 'close boarded' and measured in accordance with M60.7.2 and Measurement Rule M7.

Any overlapping of pales should be allowed in the area measured as required by Measurement Rule M2.

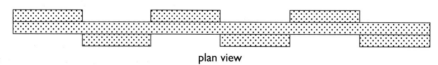

plan view

▶ Should painting to walls be measured overall with the description detailing items (i.e. pre-finished dado trunking) which are to remain unpainted?

Yes, M60.1.*.1.2, i.e. features unpainted, details stated.

▶ Would painting the fanlight section of a door frame be measured as 'to general surfaces' or as 'to glazed window/screen'?

This is measured in accordance with M60.2, 'glazed windows/screens' and both sides are measured as Measurement Rule M5.

▶ Would painting to an internal door frame be measured twice to allow for the painting operation being performed in two rooms?

No, the girth of paint to an internal frame is the total girth from one outer edge of an architrave to the outer edge of the other architrave, unless each side is painted in a different colour.

See sketch below.

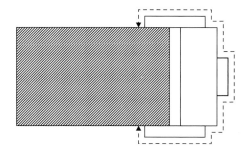

▶ Should on-site painting of furniture be measured separately from Work Section M60 'general surfaces' painting?

Yes, Work Sections N10 to N23 require the finish to be included in the item description.

▶ Should painting to log walls be measured from the bottom of the log (which is set into the ground) or from ground level?

The area measured will be the area or girth specified to be covered including allowances for edges, etc., as M60.M2.

▶ Should painting to door frames over 300mm girth be separately measured from plain general surfaces such as walls?

Yes, the application of all relevant requirements of Supplementary Information items M60.S1 to S8 inclusive to the Bill descriptions will ensure that separate items are measured.

▶ Should painting of a wall consisting of large precast concrete panels, each separated by a 12mm joint, be measured as multi-coloured work if each panel is painted a different colour?

Yes, the *Measurement Code* states on page 35 that 'the general description of the work required by General Rule 4.5 should draw attention to any known variety of colour requirements'.

▶ Should painting to a coved cornice be measured separately in linear metres if it is painted in the same type of paint as the walls and ceiling, but in a different colour?

Yes, if the cornice is of a different material than the adjacent walls and ceiling.

No, if the cornice is of the same material – but the painting description should include the words 'multi-coloured work', M60.1.*.1.1.

▶ When measuring external painting, do opening edges of metal windows include the 'hinged edge'?

The painting to opening edges is not measured. It is deemed included as stated in Coverage Rule M60.C4.(a).

The specification should make clear which opening edges are to be painted.

▶ How should the on-site painting of a timber window sill that is a component of a window that has been measured in Work Section L10 be measured?

It is measured as 'general surfaces' in accordance with M60.1.*.1–3.1–5.

▶ Does measurement of 'painting to glazed windows and glazed doors' include their frames or should the frames be measured separately?

Painting to glazed windows includes the window frame and everything else described in Coverage Rule M60.C4.

Painting to associated linings and sills is measured as general surfaces, Measurement Rule M60.M7.

Painting to glazed doors does not include the painting to their frame or lining which is measured separately as required by Measurement Rule M7.

▶ Should the painting of a recessed shadow gap around a door frame formed with plasterboard and galvanised metal angle beads be measured separately from that of the adjacent plasterboard wall if both are painted with the same type of paint?

Yes, the painting to both the recess and the metal angle would be measured separately.

Painting to a metal angle requires the base to be described, Supplementary Information item M60.S2.

As paint on the angle is measured separately, then the recess becomes isolated and must be measured in linear metres not exceeding 300mm girth.

▶ Should the painting of glazed windows and screens be separated into those with openings and those without openings?

No, the extent of opening lights should be determined from examining the drawings that must accompany the Bills of quantities, M60.P1.

▶ Should the painting of factory made windows that come to site complete with their opening gear be so described?

The Bill description should include reference to any specific items of hardware that must remain unpainted as required by item 2 in the fourth column of the Classification Table, i.e. 'features unpainted, details stated'.

▶ When measuring the painting to external rendered wall surfaces, should the painting of reveals of openings that do not exceed 300mm girth be measured separately as isolated surfaces?

Not if the type of paint and background surface is the same for both the wall and reveal.

Yes, if any matter listed in the Supplementary Information items M60.S1–S8 differs in any respect.

▶ External rendered walls are to be painted. The surface of one wall has a different texture from the other in that it is roughcast render rather than smooth render. Should separate items be measured for painting the two rendered surfaces?

Yes, Supplementary Information item M60.S2 requires the nature of the base to be given in the Bill description and General Rule 8.2 says 'where the nature of the base is required to be identified, each type of base shall be identified separately'.

▶ Structural steelwork is delivered to site having had a three coat paint system applied off site. The nuts and bolts for site assembly are unpainted. How is the painting to these bolts measured?

The painting to bolts must be measured in accordance with M60.5.1.3 as work to 'isolated areas not exceeding $0.50m^2$ irrespective of girth'.

▶ Please define the measurement of painting to open type railings.

Painting to plain open type railings is classified according to size of individual members, M60.M10. This means painting of members whose girth exceeds 300mm is measured in $m^2$ and painting to members whose girth is 300mm or less is measured in linear metres.

▶ In painting an open type steel fence, does the measurement represent one or two sides?

The painting is measured to each individual member, Measurement Rule M60.M7. Members of open type fencing whose girth is greater than 300mm are measured in m² and members whose girth is 300mm or less are measured in linear metres.

It is incorrect to measure painting in m² of each side of fence panel.

▶ Should painting to a timber window sill be measured separately as general surfaces not exceeding 300mm girth as an associated sill under Measurement Rule M7 or included in the measurement of glazed timber sash windows?

Paintwork to the sill should be measured as general surfaces, as associated linings and sills, Measurement Rule M60.M7.

The area of window to be measured for painting is defined in Measurement Rule M60.M5.

▶ Are window sills, irrespective of their construction, measurable as a general surface?

Yes.

▶ What is considered in a glazed window to be an associated lining?

It would include any lining to the reveals or sill of the opening not part of the window.

▶ How is painting a metal architrave bead around a door opening measured?

It is measured in linear metres as general isolated surfaces not exceeding 300mm girth, M60.1.*.2.

Painting to galvanised metal beads must be measured separately from any adjacent work from which it differs in any respect, as listed in Supplementary Information items M60.S1–S8.

▶ Should painting to door frames and their associated stops and architraves that exceed 300mm in girth be described as 'to isolated surfaces'?

No, only frames, etc. whose girth is less than 300mm can be described as 'isolated', M60.1.*.2.

▶ Should the measured items for redecoration works contain sufficient descriptive items to convey the full extent of the work and nature of existing backgrounds?

Yes, General Rule 4.5 requires a description to be inserted at start of each work section, stating the nature and location of work.

General Rule 1.1 requires more detailed information to be given in order to define the precise nature and extent of the work.

▶ Emulsion paint has been applied to new plastered walls and to timber beads planted onto them.

Should separate items be measured for painting the walls and beads?

Yes, separate items must be measured where backgrounds differ even if the same type of paint is applied, Supplementary Information item M60.S2.

Door frames have been painted in satin finish, though the paint on one side of the frame is different in colour from the other side.

Painting to these door frames would be described as multi-coloured work. Whether measured in linear metres or m² depends on the girth of the work.

# SMM7 Q & A

▶ Door frames are painted in the same colour over all their girth but part of them is painted in satin finish and part is painted in gloss finish.

Painting to door frames where one side is gloss and one side is satin is measured as two separate items, Supplementary Information item S6.

▶ Fencing is constructed from prefabricated panels and posts which are welded together off site and fixed together on site by bolting.

Should the works be measured as ornamental fencing or as plain open type fencing?

Painting of these railings would be measured as plain open type in accordance with M60.7.1.1–3.

▶ Where a Bill item for painting a skirting board shows 'general surfaces not exceeding 300 girth' and the skirting is 100mm high, should the painter prime the back of the skirting before fixing at no extra cost?

No, priming the back of a skirting before fixing should be measured as a separate item of painting to general isolated surfaces not exceeding 300mm girth, application on site prior to fixing as M60.1.*.2.4.

▶ Where a door frame is more than 300mm in girth, is it measured in m²?

Yes, all painting to surfaces over 300mm girth is measured in m².

▶ Measurement Rule M10 does not state a requirement for measuring plain open type fencing and gates each side.

Should only one side be measured?

No, painting to plain open type fencing is measured under M60.M10. Painting to members whose girth exceeds 300mm is measured in m², and painting to members whose girth is less than or equal to 300mm is measured in linear metres.

▶ Does multi-coloured work mean the application of more than one colour on one wall within a room?

Multi-coloured work is defined in Definition Rules M60.D2 and D3 and Coverage Rule C2.

More than one colour on any or either the walls, piers, ceilings or beams in **one** room is defined as multi-coloured work – Definition Rule M60.D3. It is **not** multi-coloured work where the walls, piers, ceilings and beams are all one colour and the woodwork is a different colour, neither is it multi-coloured work where separate rooms are painted in different colours.

▶ If a door is painted in different colours either side, would it be multi-coloured work?

A door painted in more than one colour on one face would be considered multi-coloured work but would not be considered multi-coloured work if either side is a different colour.

Does the fact that a dado rail separates the colours have any relevance?

A dado rail is irrelevant – it is the application of two or more colours in one room which defines the work as multi-coloured; Definition Rule M60.D3. Coverage Rule M60.C2 states that 'cutting in and cutting to line' is deemed included in multi-coloured work.

▶ If in a particular room three walls are painted the same colour, whilst one is painted in an alternative colour, is this defined as multi-coloured work?

Three walls one colour and one wall a different colour in one room is multi-coloured work – Definition Rule M60.D3.

If this is the case, are all the walls within the room measured and described as multi-coloured or just the one wall?

▶ Please clarify painting rules with regards to multi-coloured work:
- a single wall surface painted in more than one colour;
- a coloured band n/e 300mm wide within a wall painted in a different colour;

- walls with piers of different colours;
- walls painted in two colours where the colours are separated by a dado rail.

▶ Is the painting of one or two walls in one room (no piers) in a different colour to the other walls considered to be 'multi-coloured work'?

▶ Timber sliding sash windows and their associated parting beads have been removed from a building to enable repair work. These were painted on site before being replaced and their frames painted in situ.

How should this painting be measured?

The total area of paint to the various coloured walls within a room is grouped together and described as multi-coloured work.

These should be measured as follows:

- multi-coloured work as M60.1.*.1.1;

- the entire surface of the wall would be measured and described as multi-coloured work as M60.1.*.1.1 – the coloured band would not be measured as isolated therefore would not be measured in linear metres;
- multi-coloured work as M60.1.*.1.1;
- multi-coloured work as M60.1.*.1.1.

Yes, multi-coloured work on walls and piers or ceilings or beams as defined in Definition Rule M60.D3 means that the work is described as such if:
- one or more wall or beam is painted in a different colour than the others;
- part of a ceiling or a beam is painted in a different colour from the remaining
- part of the ceiling or the other beams.

Work is not described as multi-coloured if:
- the ceiling and beams are painted all in one colour and the walls and piers are all painted in a different colour.

The painting to sashes and parting beads would be measured and described as painted on site prior to fixing and the painting of the frame would be measured separately as an isolated surface. The painting of the sashes, parting beads and linings should be measured as:

**Sashes** – painting to glazed sash windows; application on site prior to fixing as M60.3.1–4.1.5, in m$^2$.

**Parting beads** – painting to isolated general surfaces, girth less than 300mm, application on site prior to fixing as M60.1.–.2.4, in linear metres.

**Frame/linings** – painting to general surfaces; girth over 300mm, in m$^2$ or to isolated surface less than 300mm girth as M60.1.–.1 or 2 and in accordance with Measurement Rule M60.M7, in linear metres.

# SMM7 Q & A

▶ Should caulking of joints in timber boarding general surfaces be measured or is it deemed included within the general painting item as part of the normal preparation?

Unless specific mention is made of caulking in the measured items or specification items for preparation of surfaces, caulking cannot be deemed to be included within a measured item for painting. Caulking should be measured within the Bill item for the boarding as a joint treatment as required by Supplementary Information items H20–K21.S2 or S7.

▶ Should the paint on door frames or linings be measured once full girth or twice to each side?

Painting to internal door frames, linings, architraves, etc. is girthed once and measured in m² as general surfaces over 300mm girth or in linear metres as general isolated surfaces not exceeding 300mm girth.

Painting to external door frames, linings, architraves, etc. is girthed twice, one half to be described as 'to external surfaces'.

▶ Can you clarify how painting to door frames and their associated trims is measured when there is an embedded intumescent trim in the doorstop?

The frame and trims is girthed. If over 300mm it is measured in m² and if under 300mm it is measured in linear metres.

If the frame has an intumescent insert the measurement is the same but the description should include 'features to remain unpainted'. See sketch below.

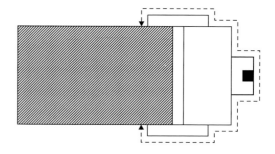

▶ Is it possible to measure cutting paint in to a line, i.e. conduit vertically, etc. or should the cutting in be included in the square metre rate, or how far does cutting in go from an inclusive point of view?

Cutting in is deemed included. The conduit will separate the wall into two separate areas. It might be appropriate to include the 'features unpainted' in the description of the wall painting as M60.1.*.1.2.

Multi-coloured to partition walls example: four walls in an office, three walls in white, one in blue. Does this qualify under multi-coloured work?

The work in this room would be described as 'multi-coloured', therefore cutting in and cutting to line is deemed included.

Generally at what point does cutting in become a variation under SMM7 and therefore measurable?

Cutting in and cutting to line are not measurable items of work. These labours are deemed included within multi-coloured work, Coverage Rule M60.C2.

# N Furniture/Equipment

▶ Where should integrated plumbing system panels be measured when not part of a proprietary partition system?

These are measured in accordance with N13.4.1.1.

▶ The drawing of a metal stud partition shows several IPS panels. The detail shows the IPS panels clipped to a 100mm x 50mm softwood subframe that is fixed to the metal studs. Would this subframe be deemed included in the Bill item for the IPS panels?

No, they should be measured as 'individual supports' in accordance with G20.13 and Definition Rule G20.D7.

▶ Would IPS (Integrated Plumbing Systems) panels for sanitary ware be classed as access panels under K10.11?

IPS panels would not be classed as access panels under K10.11. They should be measured separately in N13.4.1.1.

# P Building fabric sundries

## P10 Sundry insulation/proofing work/fire stops

▶ A loose mat insulation quilt is fixed to the underside of profiled metal roof sheeting. In which work section should the quilt be measured?

G30 is for metal decking only, insulating mats should be measured separately under P10.

▶ Should rigid mineral fibre batt fire barriers in ceiling voids be measured under Work Section K11 or P10?

This can be measured in either work section subject to provision of Measurement Rule M2 in P10. Given that the rules differ regarding the calculation of the net area the rate must therefore also differ.

▶ Should 'solar control' film to window glass be measured in Work Section P10?

No, it should be measured in Work Section L40 under the rules for 'Special glass' L40.3.1.

▶ An insulation quilt is specified to be laid between joists. When measuring the area of the quilt must the area taken up by the joists be deducted?

Yes, Measurement Rule P10.M1 states 'the area measured is that covered'.

## P20 Unframed isolated trims/skirtings/sundry items

▶ Should the decoration of joinery items that require finishing off site be measured separately from the joinery item or measured in Work Section M60?

No, the off site surface treatments applied as part of the manufacturing process should be measured with the component as Supplementary Information item L20.S3.

▶ Should the fixing of isolated timber trims with screws and pellets be so described in the measured items?

Yes, the method of fixing timber trims, when not left to the discretion of the contractor, must be given in the Bill description, Supplementary Information item P20.S8.

▶ Is the labour of scribe fitting the end of a timber skirting a measurable item?

Coverage Rule P20.C1 states that ends, angles, mitres, intersections and the like are deemed included except for hardwood items exceeding $0.003m^2$ cross sectional area.

▶ Should a skirting, cut to profile of treads and risers, be so described and measured separately from other skirtings of the same profile/section even though the Bill description stated that the work was 'in staircase areas'?

Yes, Measurement Rule P20.M1 requires sections that do not have a constant cross section to be so described.

▶ Should different items be measured for the same item of joinery trim if one piece is fixed at 400mm centres and the other piece is fixed at 600mm centres?

Yes, centres of fixings must be described when not at discretion of contractor, Supplementary Information item P20.S8.

▶ How should a skirting board or any other timber trim made up from two types of timber be described?

It should be described as a 'built-up' member, P20.1–7.1.*.1.

# P30 Trenches/Pipeways/Pits for buried engineering services

▶ How is the trench excavation measured for a situation where more than one service pipe is to be laid at different levels in the one trench?

The number and type of services to be installed in trench should be remeasured as executed and a rate calculated based on the exact circumstances which prevailed during the installation of these services.

▶ What is meant by 'nominal size' when referring to pipe sizes?

The sizes referred to in P30.1.1–2 refer to the internal diameter of pipes.

▶ How close must an existing service be to a trench excavation for an extra over time of 'next existing live services' to be measured as P30.2.4.1?

It will depend on the type of live service and the risk of the service being disturbed by the excavation process or the danger the service might present to those carrying out the excavation. If in doubt the surveyor must measure an item giving the nature of the live service, thereby allowing the contractor to fully assess the risk.

# P31 Holes/Chases/Covers/Supports for services

▶ When components such as light fittings, air diffusers or the like are not to be installed into a suspended metal lath ceiling until after the plasterwork is complete should items be measured for temporary grounds or profile pieces?

No, temporary grounds, laths, beads or the like used to set out openings to receive light fittings are not measurable.

Attendance work in connection with the fittings must be measured in accordance with the rules of Work Section P31.

▶ Where should the passing through partitions of conduits not exceeding 55mm be measured for:
(a) electrical conduit?
(b) mechanical conduit?
(c) other conduit?

These are measured in accordance with P31.20.2.1.2 except where the conduit is part of an electrical installation where individual holes are not measured, but an overall item is measured for the work in accordance with P31.19.1.*.*.

▶ Please define the measurement for BWIC in relation to cutting or forming partition holes.

Cutting or forming holes for mechanical and electrical services, pipes, conduits, etc. are measurable items and should be measured under P31.19–26 inclusive.

▶ How is the forming of slots for air conditioning grills in suspended ceiling panels measured?

Cutting or forming holes, etc. must be measured in accordance with P31.20.1.

Can the forming of these slots be deemed included in the overall item for suspended ceilings if shown on the drawings that accompany the BoQ?

No.

▶ Does SMM7 provide a definitive list of items of work that should be measured as builders' work in connection with services installations?

No, the list is not exhaustive. It is left to the discretion of the surveyor to decide. If in doubt, measure an item.

▶ When measuring holes for pipes through walls, partitions and the like, should the size of hole relate to:
  ● the size of the hole cut allowing overall size of the pipe; or
  ● the internal diameter of the pipe?

The size range referred to in P31.20.2.1 refers to the internal diameter of pipes and conduits and not the size of hole to be formed.

If a pipe is sleeved where it passes through the wall, partition, etc. does the size of hole to be measured relate to the pipe size or sleeve size?

The size measured relates to the sleeve size. The sleeve would fall into the 'and the like' in the list contained in Definition Rule P31.D7.

▶ Should cutting chases in walls for electrical conduit be measured in linear metres as P31.22.1?

No, the builder's work in connection with electrical installations is measured in accordance with P31.19.1–4.1–5.1–2. This states that builder's work in connection with electrical points is enumerated and includes the cutting of holes, mortices, sinkings and chases.

▶ Please clarify the measurement of cutting or forming holes for other services installations.

Definition Rule P31.D7 states that 'Pipes include tubes, bars, cables, conduit and the like'. Pipe sleeves are included within the 'and the like'. If the nominal size of the pipe sleeve is known when work is being measured for the BoQ, the sleeve size will be used for sizing the hole. If the size of pipe sleeve only becomes known after work has been executed, work should be remeasured as executed and the nominal size of the hole adjusted as necessary.

# Q Paving/Planting/Fencing/Site furniture

## Q10 Kerbs/Edgings/Channels/Paving accessories

▶ Should the BoQ or specification give the length of a kerb unit?

Yes, see Measurement Rule Q10.M3.

A BoQ item for kerb makes no reference to 'bedding and haunching', neither does the NBS specification item that is precisely referred to in the BoQ item. Must the contractor select supplementary information from other parts of the specification to complete Bill descriptions?

No, a specification item must be uniquely and precisely cross referenced, as required by General Rule 4.2.

If the kerb requires bedding or haunching, the details must be included in the Bill description or the specification item referred to in the Bill description.

## Q30 Seeding/Turfing

▶ A specification for grass seeding includes several specific items of preparation, i.e.

● application of compost, and

● application of fertiliser.

Should these items be measured separately or are they deemed included in the Bill description items by a specific cross reference number to the specification, i.e. Seeding, Q30/100: Preparation, Q30/101 to 120 inclusive?

The various items should be measured separately.

General Rule 4.2 does not permit aggregation of items.

## Q40 Fencing

▶ Is an end post so measured even if it is identical in shape and size to the intermediate posts?

Yes, all end posts should be considered special supports and measured 'extra over' the fencing in which they occur, as required in Q40.2.1.1.

# R  Disposal systems

## R10  Rainwater pipework/gutters

▶ How are lightning links between lengths of metal rainwater gutters and downpipes measured?

They are enumerated as extra over items in accordance with R10.2.2.1 or R10.11.2.1.

▶ Coupling pieces are used to join lengths of cast iron drainpipe together. Should these coupling pieces be measured as special joints or fittings?

Neither, they are deemed included in their running length as required by Coverage Rule R10.C3. Special joints or fittings are only measured where a joint is formed in a pipe with something that differs from those generally occurring in the running length, Definition Rule R10.D2.

## R12  Drainage below ground

▶ A manhole is to be constructed from precast concrete rings surrounded with 150mm thick, in situ concrete. It is impossible to dig a circular hole by mechanical means.

● Should the pit excavation still be measured net?

● Yes, excavation to a circular manhole should be measured net but the Bill description must make mention of the fact, therefore allowing the contractor to allow in the rates for overdig.

● Should curved earthwork support be measured?

● Yes, see D20.7, Coverage Rule C3.

● Should the formwork be measured to the concrete surround?

● Only if specified, otherwise the concrete must be described as 'poured on or against earth or unblinded hardcore'.

● Should working space allowance be measured?

● Working space would not be measured unless formwork had been used and the distance from the face of excavation and formwork is less than 600mm.

▶ A manhole pit is over 4m deep. Should the 'working space allowance' be measured to provide a safe working environment for workmen when placing the manhole base?

No, the earthwork support provides the safe working environment.

▶ When calculating the width of granular bedding below a 750mm diameter pipe with 150mm cover to both sides should an allowance be made for the thickness of the pipe walls?

No, the width would be calculated as 750mm + (2 x 150mm) = 1050mm.

▶ Should precast concrete manhole shaft rings be enumerated rather than measured in linear metres of depth?

The concrete manhole rings can be measured either by number, stating the diameter and the length of the ring or in linear metres stating the diameter.

# SMM7 Q & A

▶ Rocker joints were specified to be installed in all pipes at a distance of 750mm from the external face of manhole walls. Are these joints a measurable item?

Yes these are measurable as 'extra over' the pipework, as R12.9.1.1, or can be included in the description of building in the ends of pipes into manhole walls as R12.11.7.1 or R12.11.14.*1.

▶ When calculating the volume of rock in a pipe trench should the volume taken up by the pipe wall thickness, the earthwork support and the working space be included?

No, Measurement Rule R12.M4 describes the basis on which the volume of extra over items is calculated.

▶ Should the disposal of surplus excavated material to an off-site location be so described in the Bill description for pipe trench excavation?

Yes, R12.1.1–2.1–2.8 should make reference to this requirement.

▶ Should drainage excavation depths be described as 'average depth 1.50m, average depth 1.75m, etc.' or 'average depth between 1.50 and 1.75m, average depth between 1.75m and 2.00m'?

This should be described as average depth 1.50m, average depth 1.75m, etc.

▶ A contractor excavating pipe trenches across a landscaped site must protect client's trees. The contractor was left to assess the amount of additional handling and transporting necessary and to price and carry out the work. Should 'specified multiple handling, details stated' have been mentioned in the relevant trench excavation descriptions?

Yes, if contract documents require chestnut paling fencing be erected, a restriction has been placed on the contractor that stops him or her from executing drain trenches and disposing of excavated material at his or her discretion. If this design-imposed condition stops the contractor from placing excavated material from the pipe trench alongside the trench, the Bill description should include for 'specified multiple handling, details stated' in accordance with R12.1.1–2.1–2.7.

▶ We have a 150mm diameter drain running between two head walls with two manholes along the run, the details are as follows:
- depth of trench excavation at initial headwall – 700mm;
- length of run to first manhole – 41m;
- depth of trench at first manhole – 680mm (note – ground levels drop along drain run);
- depth of trench leaving first manhole – 680mm;
- length of run to second manhole – 20m;
- depth of trench at second manhole – 875mm;
- depth of trench leaving second manhole – 875mm;
- length of run to last headwall – 42m; and
- depth of trench at last headwall – 850mm.

Should the whole of the trench excavation be measured as 'average 750mm deep', or should an average depth be calculated for each of the three intermediate runs?

The average depth of a drain trench is calculated between manholes. Definition Rule R12.D1 states 'a run of pipe trench is an uninterrupted line of excavating such as between manholes ...'.

# Y Mechanical and electrical services measurement

## Y10 Pipelines

▶ Should the union fitting connecting two lengths of steel pipe be measured as a two-ended fitting or is it deemed included in the running length of pipe?

It should be included in the running length because everything necessary for jointing is deemed included, Y10.C1, and joints are deemed included in the running length, Y10.C3.

Should the union fitting used to join a valve to pipework be included with the measured item for that valve?

Yes, it should be included in the item for the valve because everything necessary for jointing is deemed included (Coverage Rule Y10.C1), the description of the pipework ancillary must give the method of jointing (Y10.8.1), and cutting and jointing pipes to ancillaries is deemed included in the item for that ancillary item (Coverage Rule Y10.C7).

## Y30 Air ductlines/ancillaries

▶ Should fittings that are reducing be measured extra over their larger or smaller size?

Fittings in air ductlines are measured as extra over the ducting in which they occur stating the type, Y30.2.3.1. The reducer in question would be measured giving both the smallest and largest sizes, i.e. extra over ductwork for reducer fitting.

## Y51 Testing and commissioning mechanical services

▶ How is the chlorination or similar treatment to a heating system measured?

It is measured in accordance with Y51.4.1.1. Examples of preparation can be found on page 43 of the *Measurement Code*.

## Y53 Control components – mechanical

▶ If a control valve had to be uniquely manufactured in order to comply with the contract requirements, should it be defined as such and would the description have to use any particular item?

General Rule 1.1 requires more detailed information be given, if necessary. Therefore any unique item must be fully described, giving all information required by the Supplementary Information Table plus any additional information necessary to allow the item to be fully and properly priced.

# Y60  Conduit and cable trunking

▶ Should conduit that contains bends be measured as curved conduit?

No, the definition refers to the run of the conduit between fittings. See below for examples.

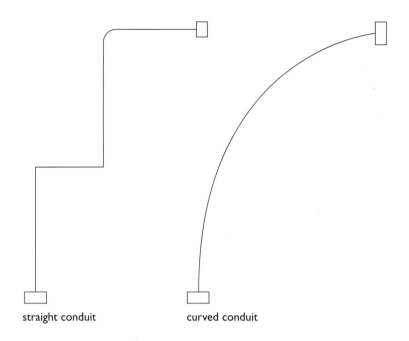

straight conduit        curved conduit

▶ In conduit and cable trunking, how are circular conduit boxes measured?

Circular conduit boxes should be measured as 'extra over the conduit in which they occur' in accordance with Y60.2.1.1.

▶ How are connections of flexible conduit to trunking measured?

They are measurable as Y60.3.4.1–2.1.

# Y61  HV/LV cables and wiring

▶ If two light points are wired from a two-gang switch, is this measured as one or two final circuits?

It is measured as two. Where the final circuits are connected to multi-gang accessories, the number of points will normally be the same as the number of gangs. See paragraphs 4 and 5 of Clause 19 on page 44 of the *Measurement Code*.